Ethnologia Europaea

Journal of European Ethnology

Volume 26 1996

MUSEUM TUSCULANUM PRESS UNIVERSITY OF COPENHAGEN

Printed in Sweden by BTJ Tryck AB, Lund 1996
ISBN 87-7289-342-7
ISSN 0425-4597

This journal is published with the support of Nordic Publication Committee for Humanist Periodicals.

Museum Tusculanum Press
University of Copenhagen
Njalsgade 92
DK-2300 Copenhagen S.

European Ethnology and Intercultural Communication

Klaus Roth

Roth, Klaus 1996: European Ethnology and Intercultural Communication. – Ethnologia Europaea 26: 3–16.

"European Ethnology" was proposed as a name of our discipline in Arnhem in 1955. Although it is now used in several European countries, it is still unclear what the name really denotes and what distinguishes it from "Folklore", "Ethnography", "Cultural Anthropology" or "Ethnology". The article attempts to determine the position of European Ethnology and to outline some of its goals and tasks: While folklorists largely focus on the study of their own, national folk cultures, and ethnologists on the study of alien, exotic cultures, European Ethnologists should concern themselves with the study of both "own" and "alien" European cultures and their interrelations and interactions, both from the emic and the etic perspectives. Thus, on the macro-level, comparative and interethnic studies should be a main concern, while on the micro-level, face-to-face inter cultural communication should become an integral object of European Ethnology. It is argued that the problems resulting from increased culture contact caused by migrations, by the European Union, by globalization etc. make the application of ethnological knowledge to the solution of these social problems indispensable – and make new demands on European Ethnologists.

Professor Dr. Klaus Roth, Institut für deutsche und vergleichende Volkskunde, Universität München, Ludwigstr. 25, D–80539 Munich, Germany.

I

The name European Ethnology appeared for the first time in 1937, as the title of a journal[1], and in 1955 it was proposed as the new name for the discipline at the International Folklore Congress in Arnhem. It was meant not only to replace the various, and partly encumbered old names like "Volkskunde", "Folklore", "Ethnography" etc., but was also to serve as a unified name in all European countries, positioning the discipline in the larger framework of ethnological sciences (cf. Lutz 1970: 29; Hauschild 1982: 11). Since then, European Ethnology has been introduced in some European countries, particularly in Scandinavia, as a name for the discipline (cf. Stoklund 1972, 1981), and it has been used in the titles of some introductions (Svensson 1973, Weber-Kellermann 1985, Brednich 1988); in addition, in spite of initial hesitation (cf. Lutz 1970), several institutes in the German speaking countries (Marburg, Frankfurt, Münster, Innsbruck, Vienna, Berlin) have since used this new name. In 1967, the journal "Ethnologia Europaea" was founded, and soon afterwards several other journals with analogous names followed.[2]

After the experience of nationalism in many European countries, the name European Ethnology was, in addition, also chosen to signal a change of perspective. In the 19th century, *Folklore or Ethnography* developed and gained legitimation as a "science of one's own people" (Lutz 1970: 27f); the interest in the description, collection, study, preservation, and often exaltation of one's *own*, 'national' (peasant) culture were its main tenets. In contrast, ethnology from its very beginning has focused on the study of *alien*, i.e., non-European "primitive" cultures. The consequence of this division of labor was that the cultural diversity of Europe, and the "otherness" of the European neighbors, remained largely unstudied, the assumption being that each country was best equipped for the study of its own folk culture. European Ethnology was meant to close this gap and to make Europe as a whole the object of ethnological research. Today, 40 years after the Arnhem congress, it is time to take stock and to ask the question: What does European Ethnology really mean, what is its relationship to folkloristics and ethnology today, and has it fulfilled the expectations, or is Leopold Kretzenbacher's sobering description of "*Ethnologia Europaea* ... as a fata morgana floating before us" (Kretzenbacher 1986: 3) still to the point? In any case, the name has as yet not been able to fully replace the old and established names of our discipline.

II

What then does European Ethnology really mean? There is general agreement that it means more and something other than simply "Ethnology in Europe", and that it does not have as its goal to set Europe as a unified "own" against the "alien" non-European world. However, apart from this, it seems there is little agreement. Instead, the existing definitions and uses of the name display a variety of views and concepts which give rise to the following critical questions:

• Is the name European Ethnology simply a synonym for the old names, a neat new label for the well-known ("folkloric", "ethnographic") subject matter? Some of the books which bear this name in their titles do not really have a European perspective (cf. Bimmer 1983, Brednich 1988, and others).

• Or, has European Ethnology developed into a mere collective name for the "European Folklores", thus preserving their national focus (Niederer 1970: 46; Lutz 1970: 28)?

• Is it perhaps the goal of European Ethnology to unify the disparate national research traditions and methods in order to create "a uniform European folklife research in systematic form" and by doing so satisfy "the need of a systematic cooperation within ethnology" (Erixon 1967: 5)? Is it its sole intent to create a forum of scholarly discourse – for the European exchange of ideas and experiences, for the discussion of theories and methods on meetings and conferences, and for the publication of these ideas in journals and omnibus volumes? Have these activities really contributed to the overcoming of the "national orientation in folkloristics that dominated in history", as Günter Wiegelmann (1977: 10) once wrote in an optimistic vein?

• Is European Ethnology a regional sub-discipline of Ethnology concerning itself with the study of Europe in the same way as regional ethnologies focus on other continents? Is it, accordingly, a discipline primarily focusing on the "other", the "alien" in Europe? The founding of a Commission for European Ethnology in the German Ethnological Society in 1993 seems to point in that direction, at least it is an attempt to overcome the division of folkloristics (*Volkskunde*) and ethnology (*Völkerkunde*) – the "dual horizon" typical of the German speaking countries which Giordano (1984: 83) deplored.

• Or is it, on the contrary, the "Ethnology of Europe", i.e., a distinct discipline, which in its approaches and methods stresses the specificity of the Old World, a discipline studying the *European* cultures in their variety and their unity? This approach, which emphasizes the special character of Europe, appears to be fairly wide-spread, particularly in the debate on development and modernization (cf. Senghaas 1982); for European Ethnology, however, it bears the risk of eurocentrism and exaltation of the own, "civilized world" (Giordano 1984: 84). Folkloristics would have failed to learn its lesson from history if, under the guise of European Ethnology, it would replace the nationalism of yesterday (cf. Gerndt 1995) with a new "European nationalism".

• Isn't European Ethnology by its very nature a *comparative* science, a "Comparative Ethnology of Europe" and above all a science of cultural relations and influences in Europe, of interdependencies and interactions between its groups and peoples?

• In other words, does European Ethnology primarily concentrate on the study of one's *own* cultures, or does it, to the same degree, also include the study of the *other* cultures in Europe, the cultures of one's neighbors and minorities, as well as those of more distant peoples and groups? Isn't it, then, a science both of the "own" and of the "other", and of the relationships between the two, of the search for identity and the experience of otherness, of the emic as well as the etic perspective?

Before we attempt a definition of the locus of European Ethnology we first have to determine the object of the discipline. Do we define "Europe" *geographically*, stretching from the Atlantic to the Ural and Caucasus Mountains in the East, and to the Bosporus in the Southeast? Or do we define it *culturally*, comprising all three "historical regions of Europe" (Szücs 1990), "culture areas" (Axt 1993) or "civilizations" (Huntington 1993)? In the latter case, do the Balkans – which often feel excluded from "Europe" (Roth 1988) – or Armenia, belong to it? And what about Turkey or the cultures of the Americas, of South Africa, Australia or Siberia that are largely outcomes of European settlement and colonization? In view of the present debate, it appears that these questions should be discussed openly in our discipline.

The founding fathers of European Ethnology wanted it not only to overcome national boundaries and limitations, but also to shed light on the coexistence of, and the interactions between the European peoples, the interrelations between the "own" and the "other" cultures, and the "near-by otherness" of neighboring countries. The name European Ethnology thus signaled a change of paradigm, a move from a narcisstic preoccupation with one's "own", to an ethnology which constantly reflects on, and incorporates the "other". The name itself was a program and a claim, and it is the premise of this paper, that neither of them have as yet been fulfilled. If we believe that the inherent program of European Ethnology is necessary and meaningful (and I am decidedly of this opinion) we are soon confronted with a number of questions concerning the specific character, the goals and methods of European Ethnology, and of course, with the question of the reasons why it has found relatively little acceptance. What should the tasks and goals of a discipline be that deserves the name European Ethnology – and what must be done to achieve these goals?

Even though European ethnologists have successfully carried out many comparative international or pan-European projects, and have studied European cultures other than their own, we cannot fail to notice that the vast majority of them concern themselves exclusively with their *own* cultures or their regional or social subcultures, usually with an "ethnocentric bias" (Niederer 1970: 46); in other words, they continue to practise ethnography or folkloristics within the boundaries of national languages, cultures, and states. They do this almost always from the inside point of view (relative to the national culture), i.e., from an *emic* perspective.[3] The necessity and the legitimacy of the study of national culture from this perspective is beyond doubt as this research serves the better understanding, and the making understandable, of one's own culture in all its complexity and dynamic change (cf. Stoklund 1972: 11). In addition, most European folklorists and ethnographers are competent only in their own culture or its subcultures. Folkloristics, as a discipline studying the national everyday culture, is of course very necessary, as long as it does not further national exaltation or the mystification and glorification of the own folk culture and history at the expense of others.

However, the study of national culture is only *one* aspect of European Ethnology and can only be a starting point for cultural understanding. This is so because of the simple fact that part of one's own culture is almost always the experience of other cultures, including the encounter with, and the management of, cultural difference: we meet the "other" as a part of our "own" already in the various regional, denominational, and social subcultures; but more importantly, the intimate neighborly contact with ethnic minorities and other peoples, with linguistic and cultural otherness, appears to be an intrinsic element of the European historical experience – at least in large parts of the continent. Indicative of this are, on the one hand, the great multiethnic states in history and the present European Union, and on the other hand, the numerous ethnically and culturally mixed areas, as well as the countries with more than one language or culture (for example Belgium, Finland, Romania, Switzerland). For many centuries, foreigners such as refugees, emigrants, settlers, merchants, journeymen, soldiers or migrant workers, have moved in large numbers to almost every European country (cf. Schuhladen 1994); the modern "guest workers" in West European countries are certainly part of that long tradition.[4] There can be no doubt that the investigation of the "other" as part of the "own", and of the processes of culture contact and acculturation should be a central task of European Ethnology.

In European folkloristics and ethnography we also find the reverse perspective: the study of the "own" as part of the "other". It was here that the older *Volkskunde* first became interested in the "other", but it was only the "islands of our own culture in a sea of alien cultures" that attracted scholarly (and political) attention. The surrounding peoples (mostly in East and Southeast Europe) were treated by this kind of "Folkloristics of Linguistic Islands" (*Sprachinselvolkskunde*) in an excluding or even disparaging manner; only the post-war "interethnic research" was able to change and correct this attitude (Weber-Kellermann 1967). After the war, some of the home countries of refugees and displaced persons were studied[5], but rarely did these studies treat both cultures in an equal way; the same holds true for most studies of European emigrants to other continents.

Judged by the total number of published works, the study of the "other", of European cultures outside one's own national or linguistic boundaries has as yet remained the exception rather than the rule for European ethnologists. In addition, many of the pertinent studies have been made from a distance, i.e., they are based on the evaluation of literary or similar sources, and not, or only to a small extent, on empirical work. However, it is precisely the exposure to foreign cultures which furthers the understanding not only of these cultures but also of one's own culture. It was Wilhelm Heinrich Riehl who emphasized the intrinsic value of studying foreign cultures in his essential paper on "Die Volkskunde als Wissenschaft" [*Folklore as a Science*] as early as in 1858. He wrote (Riehl 1910: 207f): "Only he who has been abroad is able to perceive and describe his home country in an objective manner; by its very nature, Folklore is comparative, and from the comparative observation it develops its laws, and the genuine student of the folk does not travel around only in order to depict what is out there, but also to gain the proper perspective for the conditions in his home country." In 1970, Arnold Niederer stressed the necessity of experiencing the "other" for this "proper perspective" on the "own" with these words: "Indeed, the specific problems of one's own culture remain unproblematic, if they are not clarified through the comparison with other cultures" (Niederer 1970: 46).

The study of other (European) cultures or culture areas (from the *etic* perspective of the researcher as a *professional stranger*[6]) in the framework of a so-defined European Ethnology is guided by a diversity of research interests, approaches, and perspectives. I will indicate the most important ones:

1. There are several reasons why the study of national cultures by foreign researchers has remained relatively rare. Apart from the above mentioned intrinsic orientation of the discipline, the lack of knowledge of languages and cultures, as well as other factors, among them the fact that large parts of Eastern Europe were inaccessible to foreign scholars over long periods, must be held responsible. For some European regions – like the Balkans – it has been said that "with their diversity of languages, cultures, religions, denominations, political and mental changes, constraints, and hopes they have hardly ever been in the focus of German folkloristics" and will "continue to remain difficult to access because of the barriers of languages and political systems" (Kretzenbacher 1986: 3). The 'political system' Kretzenbacher had in mind has since disappeared ...

It is indicative and at the same time surprising that the folkloristic or ethnological studies by foreign scholars only rarely concern neighboring countries with related cultures or the larger industrialized countries of Central and Western Europe. In countries like France, England, Switzerland, or Germany only a handful of North American cultural anthropologists have ventured to do research (Theodoratus 1982); it has to be stressed, though, that the contribution of English and American social and cultural anthropologists to European Ethnology is remarkable (cf. ibid; Lange 1970, Stoklund 1972: 9–11). However, the rule of ethnological research in Europe is that ethnologists or folklorists from industrialized European countries[7], or the USA[8], study relict cultures in the peripheral, "exotic" regions of Europe, like the Mediterranean countries, particularly Southern Italy and Spain, the Balkans (cf. Roth 1993b), Ireland, Scotland or other marginal areas – sometimes in cooperation with native colleagues (cf. Hofer 1968).

2. *All-European studies*, i.e., studies covering all of Europe or at least large sections of it and treating them as one large cultural area, have rarely been conducted by folklorists (cf. Cuisenier 1979); if so, they usually limit themselves to very narrow thematic units like family forms (Gavazzi 1979/80), instruments of carrying (Kłodnicki 1982/83), threshing flails (Trojan 1983) or carriages (Viires 1977/78). More comprehensive and courageous treatments of larger cultural complexes have as yet emerged only from related disciplines like Cultural or Intellectual History (cf. Burke 1978).

3. *Parallel studies* are more frequent. In these studies, native researchers investigate and treat the same subject parallelly in their own (European) countries, usually without attempting a comparison. The approach gains a European dimension only through a later synopsis of the results in a larger framework, as is the case with such endeavors as the atlas projects in various European countries and the attempts at their synopsis[9], but also the volumes on the folk cultures of the European countries (cf. Gebhard 1963), on food and food research in Europe (*Ethnologia Europaea* 5), on community studies (*Ethnologia Europaea* 6), on nationalism (*Ethnologia Europaea* 19), and on mythologies (*Ethnologia Europaea* 21).

4. *Comparative studies*, by contrast, explicitly focus on the comparison of cultures or culture elements, i.e., on the search for differences or similarities between two or more European cultures. It seems natural for European Ethnology as an essentially comparative science that comparisons play a vital role (cf. Gerndt 1977/78), be it the comparison of folk tale variants for the determining of ecotypes according to the historical-geographic method[10], be it the comparison of specific elements of folk culture (cf. Baumgarten 1983), or be it the comparison of national cultures, culture areas or little communities (cf. Bianco 1974).

5. Studies of the *relationships* and *interdependencies* between cultures and of the *interethnic relations* in Europe are of a different nature: they concern either the macro level of entire peoples or nations, or the micro level of regions, communities or groups. On the macro level, we have studies of the migration of folk tales (by the Finnish School), of cultural influences (cf. Schier 1966) and boundaries (cf. Weiss 1962), of processes of diffusion, migration or remigration (Burkard 1993), but in the same group we also have studies of the perceptions of peoples or nations of themselves and of the stereotypical images they have of others (cf. Gerndt 1988). On the micro level we have studies of interethnic relations in ethnically mixed areas or communities like the ones carried out in Southeast Europe by Ingeborg Weber-Kellermann and Annemie Schenk, as well as the more recent studies in villages or cities focusing on the relations between migrant workers and the indigenous population (cf. Greverus 1988).

6. Finally, *interactional studies* are located entirely on the micro level of personal contacts between members of different cultures. In these investigations of intercultural communication the focus is on direct culture contact and culture conflict[11], i.e., on personal interactions and *face-to-face* communications as well as on aspects that are relevant for them like the perception and understanding of the self (cf. Daun 1996), the perception and interpretation of the "other" (Niederer 1970), and on cultural differences and how to deal with them. While there already is a number of relevant ethnological studies from Scandinavia (cf. Ehn 1993, Daun 1989, 1996, Tuomi-Nikula 1993), they are as yet relatively rare in other European countries (cf. Roth 1993a, Volbrachtová 1988).

III

Unlike the traditional names of the discipline, European Ethnology thus denotes and implies above all a science of the diversity of European peoples and cultures and of their coexistence and interrelations; more precisely: of the cultures *in* Europe, because by necessity the cultures of non-European migrants and refugees now living in Europe have to be covered by the discipline as well. In summing up, European Ethnology is no longer exclusively a science of the own culture, but also – and essentially – a science of interrelations and interactions between one's "own" and the "other". This is so for the simple reason that today the "own" and the "other" can no longer be separated from each other so clearly – if they ever could. It is no coincidence, then, that the boundaries between folkloristics and ethnology begin to disappear and that the latter moves closer to European Ethnology.

The research tasks and goals of European Ethnology can thus be defined on the one hand, and in accordance with Günter Wiegelmann's view (1977: 9f), as the documentation, description, and classification of the material, social and spiritual cultures of the diverse groups and peoples living in Europe, and as the analysis of their changing expressive forms, norms and values; on the other hand, the tasks of the discipline must also include the study of these cultures in their interrelations and of the dynamics of their coexistence, their contacts and their conflicts.

While this claim to European Ethnology may be satisfied to some extent by ethnological research, this is certainly not yet true for teaching and practical application. Inevitably, the question arises as to what the purpose of ethnological research is. Isn't it also a task of European Ethnology to hand some of the vast accumulated knowledge back to those from whom it was gathered? Isn't it the duty of the discipline to contribute to the solving of social problems as was demanded at the Falkenstein conference[12] some 25 years ago? Naturally, many folklorists and ethnologists will feel uneasy at the thought of an "applied European Ethnology", because they remember the dangers involved in the application of cultural knowledge, be it by politicians or administrators, by clerics or ideologists, by businessmen or the military. The fear that ethnologists or ethnological knowledge will be used for an unethical cause is certainly not unfounded, as the war in former Yugoslavia has again demonstrated.

Thus, we must wonder what the contribution of ethnological knowledge to the solution of what social problems can be. We have to know who can misuse this knowledge for what purposes, and how to prevent this misuse. However, the fear of misuse must not paralyze European Ethnologists, because they must be aware of the fact that our societies are presently (again) plagued with grave social problems, problems that concern, and challenge, our discipline in a very special way. While, for a number of decades it looked like ethnic conflicts in Europe were a matter of the past and that wars were unthinkable, we are now witnessing a frightening growth of ethnic self awareness, "cultural racism" and cultural fundamentalism, the "ethnification" of social and political conflicts and a new nationalism, and an ominous flaring up of interethnic conflicts (cf. Köstlin 1994, Kaschuba 1995). After the "end of systems", there are conflicts mostly along the old fault lines between the three major European culture areas (cf. Szücs 1990, Axt 1993, Huntington 1993). Furthermore, in many West European countries, the influx of migrant workers, refugees, and asylum seekers as well as a popular skepticism towards the European Union has given rise to national, regional and ethnic particularisms. If we add the growing internationalization of all spheres of political, economic and social life and the increased number of culture contacts in everyday life, it appears that cultural difference has again become a problem. The sociologist Robert Picht pointed out in 1987, that with the intensification of international cooperation, the "cultural wall" will grow, because "alienness, this seemingly impenetrable and irritating strangeness of mentalities and orientations, is all the more perceptible, the more the partners are dependent on each other" (Picht 1987: 282). Today, millions of people are, to an almost unprecedented degree, expected to manage cultural diversity in everyday life. Neither the people, nor the relevant disciplines, among them European Ethnology, seem to be in a position to actively contribute to the overcoming of the "cultural walls" and to the "reconciliation of differences" (Adorno 1951: 130).

What is the attitude of European Ethnologists toward these obviously increasing social problems? Will they continue to be the keepers and preservers of their own national cultures? Will they stand on the side of those who follow the arguments of cultural nationalism and ethnocentrism, of those who demand cultural homogeneity and may even legitimize ethnic cleansings? Such attitudes are certainly incompatible with everything the name European Ethnology stands for. Never again must it go the way "applied folkloristics" went, or was forced to go, in the service of nationalistic or socialist ideologies or party programs (cf. Jacobeit et al. 1994, Gerndt 1995). But can it, in order to avoid this danger, be the position of European Ethnologists to cautiously stand at the sidelines, to remain an observing and analyzing neutral third party, and deny their contribution to the reduction of interethnic tensions and culture conflicts in Europe? In view of the nature and seriousness of the problems this can hardly be the adequate position.

In order to satisfy these demands, European Ethnology has to become serious about the change of its paradigms. Although all the well-established activities will continue to be necessary, it will no longer suffice to merely organize international meetings and conferences, to publish journals covering Europe or larger regions of it[13], to engage in comparative studies in cooperation with European colleagues, or to do occasional research in other European cultures. Today, European Ethnology is expected to come up with more far-reaching concepts and activities which will, however, make higher demands on all persons involved:

1. With its treasure of knowledge about the cultures and peoples of Europe and the relations and influences between them, European Ethnology is required to make this knowledge available in order to reduce damages and to further the communication and understanding between ethnic groups and nations. It should do its share to increase the competence of people to cope with cultural difference and diversity, and it should point out ways to a better understanding and cooperation between European peoples and nations. This would constitute an "applied European Ethnology" in the service of a more fruitful and even synergetic coexistence of groups and peoples in a world that has become smaller, a world of globalization and of growing culture contacts in almost all spheres of live – from business, trade and politics to cultural relations and mass tourism.

How can European Ethnology achieve this goal of furthering interethnic cooperation and understanding? What will have to change? For the sake of its role in contemporary society, it has to develop new directions in research and teaching. Departing from the study of their own culture, European Ethnologists have to overcome the (still very relevant) national boundaries in favor of more comprehensive and problem oriented approaches. In doing this, European Ethnology should not deny the relevance of cultural differences (cf. Schiffauer 1996) and contribute to a unified culture: The diversity of European cultures is the basis, and to safeguard it is the goal of this discipline. But if this diversity should not unfold a destructive potential, it is inevitable to share knowledge and to teach cultural techniques for the successful management of diversity and otherness. In other words, it must be the goal of applied European Ethnology to facilitate communication between culturally diverse groups or individuals and to help them accept cultural differences and to learn how to deal with them in a positive way in everyday life (cf. Roth 1996).

2. From these general reflections follow some concrete consequences for those who do ethnological research and for those who teach and study European Ethnology at the university. For more and more university teachers, the competence in another European culture, i.e., the theoretical and practical knowledge of another language and culture will become a prerequisite. This should result in more lectures and seminars, but also in more research on these cultures; in particular, cross-cultural research projects will be needed, projects which

explicitly incorporate both the emic and the etic perspectives and thereby demand the close cooperation of native and foreign colleagues (cf. Hofer 1968). On the level of institutions it will be vital to increase and intensify the cooperations between European university and research institutes as well as the exchange of university teachers in the context of European mobility programs.

The same demands will apply to the students of European Ethnology, for whom the acquiring of intimate knowledge of at least one other European culture (with stress on everyday culture and on language) will become a prerequisite. This knowledge should be gained on the theoretical level through lectures and courses, and on the practical level through the participation in structured excursions and visits to the respective country, but mostly through exchange programs with other European universities (within the framework of European mobility programs) or through internships abroad.

In view of the ethnic, cultural, religious, and linguistic diversity of Europe it must, in addition, be the goal of our discipline to enhance the understanding of other cultures by making the accumulated knowledge about these cultures available to the public. In almost all countries, the vast majority of ethnological research is published in the national language; for most European countries this means that they are read almost exclusively by small national audiences of scholars and laymen. An urgent task of European Ethnology should be to produce comprehensive bibliographies of individual cultures or culture areas comprising all the existent literature in all major European languages, to make research accessible across linguistic boundaries[14], as well as to create data bases with information about individual cultures.[15]

IV

The most active and immediate contribution of European Ethnology to the better understanding between peoples, however, would be the incorporation of Intercultural Communication into its domains of research, teaching, and application (cf. Roth 1993a). Intercultural Communication, which closely relates the two basic concepts of "culture" and "communication", is the science of the communicative interactions and exchanges of meanings between members of different cultures, of the perception and interpretation of the "other", and of the management of cultural differences (cf. Hinnenkamp 1994).

Intercultural Communication has emerged from several disciplines and is, by its nature and origin, interdisciplinary. Its methods, theories, and approaches are derived from (a) cultural anthropology, to which it owes its theoretical and methodological basis, from (b) Speech and Communication and pragmatic linguistics which contributed largely through the fields of text hermeneutics and discourse analysis, from (c) cross-cultural psychology with its valuable insights into human perception, identity, and the coping with cultural otherness, and from (d) intercultural education. Folkloristics and ethnography have also made invaluable contributions in important fields such as interethnic relations, migration, enculturation and acculturation, stereotypes, ritual, everyday narration, as well as in other related areas.

Both *culture* and *communication* are systems of symbolic interaction and exchange of meaning; by virtue of this they are closely related or almost synonymous with each other. For practical reasons, though, I will discuss the two separately.

The very basis of Intercultural Communication is the broad concept of 'culture' which – and this is vital in this context – comprises both the visible objectivations (artifacts, actions, behaviors) and the invisible subjectivations, i.e., the values and norms, attitudes and assumptions, ideas and concepts, ways of thinking and patterns of perception. Cultures are viewed as historical, dynamic, complex and highly differenciated systems. With regard to the question as to whether cultures have to be understood as *cognitive systems* (like languages) with their own "grammars", as W. H. Goodenough maintains, or as *symbolic systems*, as Clifford Geertz maintains, I believe a middle position should be taken which combines both approaches.

Both in research and in teaching, Intercultural Communication is confronted with the gap and the tension between the actual complexity of cultural systems and human behavior, and the (necessary) human tendency to reduce this complexity in the perception and to create simple categories. Thus, on the one hand, we have to deal with the complexity and dynamism of cultural macro systems (like national cultures) with all their subsystems (like regional, class, group, gender cultures etc.), while on the other hand we are faced with the human inclination to create and pass on simplified stereotypical "images in the head" of one's own and of other groups and peoples. For actual encounters between individuals from different cultures, it does not so much matter how the other culture or its representatives "really" are, but how they are perceived and how these perceptions are interpreted and determine real actions. Fortunately, for the interpretation of the behavior and actions of a member of another culture, we usually do not need *all* the existing information about the *entire* culture, but must only know its basic assumptions and typical norms and values which bear on large sectors of real behavior.

Thus, Intercultural Communication has to concern itself intensely with the typical patterns of perception and of interpretation, with attribution and stereotyping, and with the use of stereotypes. It must fully consider the micro cultural or individual variation and the dynamics of symbolic social interaction, as well as determine the basic values and norms, concepts and standards of each culture, in a sense the basic elements of its "grammar".[16]

The second pillar of Intercultural Communication is *communication* in both its functions as exchange of meanings and as symbolic social interaction. In the case of communication between strangers, the *relational aspect* (Watzlawick 1967) gains special significance over the *contential aspect* for the outcome of this interaction. This is so because the larger part of meaning is not transmitted verbally (and thus more on the cognitive level), but para-verbally (intonation, speed, pauses etc.) and above all nonverbally and extra-verbally (through gestures, body language, behavior etc.). Intercultural communication and understanding is therefore very much dependent on the decoding of nonverbal signals, i.e., of the (largely affective) human behavior outside language. Beyond the decoding of verbal denotations and connotations, intercultural communication thus involves to a large extent the deciphering of unfamiliar *actions* and their underlying norms and assumptions.

Intercultural Communication as a relational science is thus not so much concerned with the *comparison* of cultures but with concrete *interactions*. Its main question is: What happens when individuals with different cultural codes socially interact and communicate. Culture contact, culture conflict, culture shock, understanding and misunderstanding between members of different cultures are therefore the central problems of Intercultural Communication.

Various approaches have been developed and applied to the problem of diverging cultural codes and of cultural variation. In spite of the basic problem, both of intercultural communication and of intercultural research and teaching, that every person, including the scholar, always perceives and evaluates other cultures through his or her own "cultural lenses", it is nevertheless a fundamental demand on Intercultural Communication to take a neutral position between the cultures and to make *cultural relativism* its basis. But it is exactly the position of relativism which presupposes a *fixed point* and a common denominator from which the diversity of cultures can be grasped and made comparable. All extant theoretical approaches to intercultural communication agree in that they set this fixed point outside culture, in the universals of human nature. Departing from the assumption that (1) "there is a limited number of common human problems for which all peoples at all times must find some solutions," that (2) "while there is variability in solutions of all the problems, it is neither limitless nor random but is definitely variable within a range of possible solutions", and that (3) "all alternatives of all solutions are present in all societies at all times but are differentially preferred," the anthropologists Florence Kluckhohn and F.L. Strodtbeck in 1961 determined five such basic problems of humankind. They stated these problems in the form of questions to which each culture finds its own answers:

(1) What is the character of innate human nature? (*human nature orientation*), (2) What is the relation of man to nature (and supernature)? (*man-nature orientation*), (3) What is the temporal focus of human life? (*time orientation*), (4) What is the modality of human activity? (*activity orientation*) and (5) What is the modality of man's relationship to other men? (*relational orientation*). With regard to "man–nature orientation" they discern, for example, the three basic variations "subjugation to nature", "harmony with nature" and "mastery over nature", while "time orientation" has the three basic variations "past", "present", and "future orientation" (Kluckhohn 1961: 10–12).

Departing from the findings of proxemics and linguistics, the cultural anthropologist Edward T. Hall as early as in 1959 developed a model according to which culture consists of ten *primary message systems*. These interrelated and interdependent information systems are founded in biology and human nature. Each of these message systems[17] is culturally modified and value-laden. Hall focused on the message systems of territoriality (attitude to space), temporality (attitude to time), interaction, and association, and made such helpful distinctions as those between *high-context* and *low-context* cultures or between cultures with a *monochronic* or *polychronic* use of time: in high-context cultures there are dense networks of social relations and information, whereas in low-context cultures the density and flow of information is considerably lower; people in monochronic cultures usually do "one thing after the other", while in polychronic cultures people tend to do several things at the same time. These basic orientations influence large sectors of the entire cultural system and of individual behavior. It is one of Hall's core messages that language is a part of only one out of ten information systems (*interaction*) and that it belongs to the visible part of the *cultural iceberg*, while the much larger non-verbal "hidden culture" remains invisible to the eye.

In 1980, on the basis of over one hundred thousand questionaires completed in 40 countries, the Dutch organizational psychologist Geert Hofstede was able to determine four basic factors which largely govern human behavior at the work place. However, due to their deep-rootedness, these factors can serve as key indicators far beyond work relations, because they influence the answers to basic questions of human existence, and therefore influence many sectors of the cultural system. The four key cultural indicators are (1) the *Power Distance Index*, which refers to the fact that each culture deals with the given uneven distribution of power and wealth in a different manner and creates and tolerates different kinds of social hierarchies and distribution of power, (2) the *Uncertainty Avoidance Index*, which indicates the different attitudes to the risks of human life in each culture; cultures with a high risk avoidance tend to favor rules, rites, traditions, and security, (3) the *Individualism Index*, which indicates the different degrees of social cohesion and the relative strength of individualism or collectivism in a given culture, and (4) the *Masculinity Index,* which is an indicator of the culturally defined roles and properties of the genders and also refers to the "masculinity" or "femininity" of whole cultures (Hofstede 1980, 1991).

Given the limitations of this paper, it is impossible to discuss in detail the theoretical foundations of Intercultural Communication.[18] Instead, I will conclude with a few remarks on how all these (and many other) theoretical and empirical findings are used for teaching Intercultural Communication at the University of Munich (cf. Roth 1996). In a joint project of the disciplines folkloristics (*Volkskunde*), ethnology (*Völkerkunde*) and German as a Foreign Language over the past six years, we have developed and tested concepts for the teaching of Intercultural Communication with a strong focus on ethnology and cultural anthropology. The primary goal is the creation of *intercultural competence*, i.e., the conveying of *cultural awareness*, of knowledge about, and sensitivity toward, one's own and other cultures. This implies a decision for the *culture general* and not for the *culture specific* approach. The first is well tested and is, in our opinion, the most adequate one for the ethnological sciences[19]; it does not aim at individual cultures, but rather at conveying general knowledge about culture, communication, perception and stereotyping, hermeneutics, and the management of cultural differences. Individual cultures are, of course, dealt with in the discussions of concrete intercultural interactions and conflicts, and apart from that, the students are encouraged to acquire (in other disciplines) factual knowledge about individual cultures and languages, and to gain practical cultural competence in the relevant countries. These goals can be reached by different didactic means. As to the question whether a *cognitive* or *affective* approach is better suited for university students or adults, our experience shows that for the teaching of intercultural knowledge and competences the cognitive approach with the inclusion of some affective elements produces good results; at the university level, too much experiental and affective-emotional learning can be problematic (Roth 1992).

The indicated didactic approach consists of the following phases: In the first phase, the foundations of culture and communication theory are taught and the students are made aware of their own culture and of the degree to which their patterns of perception, attribution, and interpretation are determined by it. Making students aware of their "cultural lenses" is the prerequisite for the second phase, in which the interpretation and understanding of cultural "otherness" are treated, if possible on the basis of personal experiences. This means that the theoretical and practical development of awareness for cultural difference, for hidden signals, and for the logic of unfamiliar behaviors and actions are part of the curriculum. In the third phase the attempt is made to develop the capacity to adequately interact and communicate with members of other cultures, i.e., to teach techniques for dealing with other cultural codes. The development of empathy and of the ability to change perspectives is a precondition for successful mediation and solving of intercultural conflicts and for the creation of cultural synergy. In the fourth phase, the acquisition of knowledge about specific cultures or countries (including the topography, history, language, literature, institutions etc.) and the application of the theoretical knowledge to concrete intercultural contexts and research problems forms a central part of the program.

V

The specific tasks of European Ethnology do not only result from the increased gravity of ethnic problems at the end of our century (cf. Köstlin 1994), but rather from the historical realities of Europe. It is these realities which demand a synthesis of approaches of all ethnological disciplines, a combination of the study of one's own and of other (European) cultures, the incorporation of the emic and the etic as well as of the diachronic and the synchronic perspectives. The occupation with the problems of cultural diversity, of coexistence and influences, of relations and conflicts between the European peoples and ethnic groups, but also of intercultural communication between individuals – all this constitutes the specific appeal and the opportunity of European Ethnology. For these tasks it is not only well-equipped, but as a discipline engaged in the study of European cultures, it also has the duty to contribute to the solving of problems arising from cultural diversity and increased culture contact. Like no other discipline it can take into account both the specific historical conditions and the present complex ethnic and cultural situation in Europe. It would be very helpful if both the national and the international associations of European ethnologists[20] and the supranational institutions would react to this challenge in a more pronounced way. By doing so, they could certainly give new impulses to teaching and research – and thereby furnish the discipline with a new and fitting profile and open new fields of professional activity for young European ethnologists, for example as mediators between cultures.[21]

Notes

Translation and revision by the author of: Europäische Ethnologie und Interkulturelle Kommunikation. In: *Schweizerisches Archiv für Volkskunde* 91 (1995) 163-181. I am grateful to Rachel Baron, Munich, for her comments on the English translation.

All translations of quotations in this article are by the author.

1. In 1937, Sigurd Erixon published the first issue of *Folkliv* with the subtitle *Review of Nordic and European Ethnology*; in 1938, the name was changed to *Journal for European Ethnology and Folklore* (v. Bringéus 1983: 229f).
2. *Ethnologia Slavica* [1969], *Ethnologia Scandinavica* [1971], *Ethnologie française* [1971], *Ethnologia Fennica* [1972], *Ethnologia Polona* [1975]; on this problem see Wiegelmann 1977: 9.
3. From the fact that folklorists favored the "inner exotism", i.e., the study of marginal regions and lower social classes (like peasants) in their own countries, and that the scholars almost exclusively came from urban bourgeois milieus, it follows that there always existed a certain *etic* perspective in folkloristic research.
4. Cf. Palairet 1987, and the numerous studies of migrant workers made at the Frankfurt Institut für Kulturanthropologie.
5. E.g. by Alfred Cammann, Alfred Karasek, Josef Hanika and others.
6. Cf. Michael Agar: The Professional Stranger. New York 1980.
7. Of the German speaking scholars one should mention: Maximilian Braun, Dagmar Burkhart, Christian Giordano, Ina-Maria Greverus, Leopold Kretzenbacher, Max Matter, Arnold Niederer, Klaus Roth, Rudolf Schenda, Werner Schiffauer, Alois Schmaus, Claudia Schöning-Kalender, Gabriella Schubert, Ingeborg Weber-Kellermann, Gisela Welz.
8. If we take the works by American cultural anthropologists on European cultures listed in Theodoratus' bibliography (1982: 154-162) as an example, some 75% concern the Balkans, Spain, Southern Italy, Ireland/Scotland, and Russia, and only some 25% deal with the remaining European countries.
9. E.g. the volume edited by Matthias Zender and the Permanent International Atlas Commission *Forschungen zum ethnologischen Atlas Europas und seiner Nachbarländer, vol. 1: Die Termine der Jahresfeuer in Europa – Erläuterungen zur Verbreitungskarte*. Göttingen: Schwartz 1980.
10. A case in point are the numerous monographs on tale or ballad types, most of which have been published in Helsinki in the renowned series *Folklore Fellows Communications*.
11. E.g. between members of ethnic groups or migrant workers (cf. Gyr 1989), at the work place in institutions and organizations (cf. Roth 1993a), among expatriates or in intercultural marriages (Tuomi-Nikula 1993).
12. Cf. Wolfgang Brückner (ed.): Volkskunde in Deutschland. Begriffe – Probleme – Tendenzen. Diskussion zur Standortbestimmung. Frankfurt am Main 1970.
13. Like the *Anthropological Journal on European Cultures* [1992ff], *Ethnologia Europaea, Ethnologia Scandinavica, Ethnologia Slavica, Ethnologia Balkanica,* and others.
14. For Southeastern Europe cf. Roth 1993b.
15. The Institute of Folklore at the Bulgarian Academy of Sciences is establishing (with the support of UNESCO) a "Data Base of Balkan Folklore" which is to contain analytical data on the spiritual, social, and material culture of seven Balkan countries; the data bases are to be made available on CD roms.
16. For the contemporary Swedish culture cf. Åke Daun 1989 and other papers in the same volume of *Ethnologia Europaea*.
17. Hall's ten Primary Message Systems are *interaction, association, subsistence, bisexuality, territoriality, temporality, learning, play, defense, exploitation* (Hall 1973: 95).
18. Apart from the literature already quoted see Dodd 1991, Desjeux 1991, Samovar 1991, Hofstede 1991, Hansen 1995, Hinnenkamp 1994: 1–25.
19. As well as for Speech and Communication, Linguistics, Education, Psychology and other disciplines.
20. Like *Ethnologia Europaea*, the Société internationale d'ethnologie et folklore (SIEF) with its commissions, and others.
21. The ethnologist as a "marginal man" is in any case predestined "for the role of an interpreter, arbiter and mediator" and his activity has "again and again been compared to that of the translator or interpreter" (Lindner 1989: 24).

References

Adorno, Theodor 1951: *Minima moralia*. Frankfurt.

Axt, Heinz-Jürgen 1993: Die Befreiung der Kulturen. Europas Kulturkreise nach dem "Ende der Systeme". In: *Südosteuropa-Mitteilungen* 33: 1–13.

Baumgarten, Karl 1983: Das englische und das deutsche Hallenhaus – Versuch einer Deutung. In: *Ethnologia Europaea* 13: 189–202.

Bianco, Carla 1974: *The Two Rosettos*. Bloomington.

Bimmer, Andreas C. (ed.) 1983: *Europäische Ethnologie in der beruflichen Praxis. Berichte aus Museum und Hochschule*. Bonn: Habelt.

Brednich, Rolf W. (ed.) 1988: *Grundriß der Volkskunde. Einführung in die Forschungsfelder der Europäischen Ethnologie*. Berlin: Reimer.

Bringéus, Nils-Arvid 1983: The Predecessors of Ethnologia Europaea. In: *Ethnologia Europaea* 13: 228–233.

Burkard, Maria 1993: *Entre dos tierras – Zwischen zwei Welten. Transkulturationsprozeß galicischer RemigrantInnen*. M.A. thesis Tübingen.

Burke, Peter 1978: *Popular Culture in Early Modern Europe*. London.

Cuisenier, J. (ed.) 1979: *Europe as a Cultural Area*. The Hague: Mouton.

Daun, Åke 1989: Studying National Culture by Means of Quantitative Methods. In: *Ethnologia Europaea* 19: 25-32.

Daun, Åke 1996: Swedish Mentality. University Park, PA: Penn. State University Press [= *Svensk mentalitet.* Stockholm 1990].

Desjeux, Dominique 1991: *Le sens de l'autre. Stratégies, réseaux et cultures en situation interculturelle*. Paris: UNESCO.

Dodd, Carley H. 1991: *Dynamics of Intercultural Communication*. Dubuke: Wm.C.Brown Publishers.

Ehn, Billy, Jonas Frykman, Orvar Löfgren 1993: *Försvenskningen av Sverige. Det nationellas förvandlingar*. Stockholm: Natur och Kultur.

Erixon, Sigurd 1967: European Ethnology in Our Time. In: *Ethnologia Europaea* 1: 3–11.

Gavazzi, Milovan 1979/80: Die Mehrfamilien der europäischen Völker. In: *Ethnologia Europaea* 11: 158–190.

Gebhard, Torsten, Josef Hanika 1963: *IRO-Volkskunde. Europäische Länder*. Munich: IRO-Verlag.

Gerndt, Helge 1977/78: Die Anwendung der vergleichenden Methode in der Europäischen Ethnologie. In: *Ethnologia Europaea* 10: 2–32.

Gerndt, Helge 1988 (ed.): *Fach und Begriff "Volkskunde" in der Diskussion*. Darmstadt: WBG.

Gerndt, Helge (ed.) 1988: *Stereotypvorstellungen im Alltagsleben. Beiträge zum Themenkreis Fremdbilder – Selbstbilder – Identität*. Festschrift für G. Schroubek. München.

Gerndt, Helge 1995: Deutsche Volkskunde und Nationalsozialismus – was haben wir aus der Geschichte gelernt? In: *Schweiz. Archiv für Volkskunde* 91: 53–75.

Greverus, Ina-Maria et al. (eds.) 1988: *Kulturkontakt – Kulturkonflikt*. 2 vols. Frankfurt/M.

Giordano, Christian 1984: Soziologie, Ethnologie, Kulturanthropologie. Zur Bestimmung wissenschaftlicher Horizonte. In: *Kulturanthropologie und Europäische Ethnologie in Frankfurt*, ed. Institut für Kulturanthropologie ... Frankfurt/M., 79–90.

Gyr, Ueli 1989: *Lektion fürs Leben. Welschlandaufenthalte als traditionelle Bildungs-, Erziehungs- und Übergangsmuster*. Zürich.

Hall, E.T. 1959: *The Silent Language*. Garden City, NY.

Hall, Edward T. 1969: *The Hidden Dimension*. Garden City, NY: Anchor Books.

Hansen, Klaus P. 1995: *Kultur und Kulturwissenschaft*. Tübingen, Basel: Francke.

Hauschild, Thomas 1982: Zur Einführung – Formen europäischer Ethnologie. In: Nixdorf/Hauschild (eds.): *Europäische Ethnologie,* 11–26.

Hinnenkamp, Volker 1994: *Interkulturelle Kommunikation*. Heidelberg (Studienbibliographien Sprachwissenschaft).

Hofer, Tamás 1968: Anthropologists and Native Ethnographers in Central European Villages: Comparative Notes on the Professional Personality of the Disciplines. In: *Current Anthropology* 9: 311–315.

Hofstede, Geert 1980: *Culture's Consequences: International Differences in Work-Related Values*. Beverly Hills, London: Sage.

Hofstede, Geert 1991: *Interkulturelle Zusammenarbeit. Kulturen – Organisationen – Management*. Wiesbaden: Gabler.

Huntington, Samuel P. 1993: Clash of Civilizations? In: *Foreign Affairs* 72,3: 22–49.

Jacobeit, Wolfgang, Hannjost Lixfeld, Olaf Bockhorn (eds.) 1994: *Völkische Wissenschaft. Gestalten und Tendenzen der deutschen und österreichischen Volkskunde in der ersten Hälfte des 20. Jhs.* Wien.

Kaschuba, Wolfgang 1995: Kulturalismus: Vom Verschwinden des Sozialen im gesellschaftlichen Diskurs. In: *Zeitschrift für Volkskunde* 91: 27–46.

Kłodnicki, Zygmunt et al. 1982/83: Zur Systematik der Dreschflegel in Europa. In: *Ethnologia Europaea* 13: 85–96.

Kluckhohn, Florence and F.L. Strodtbeck 1961: *Variations in Value Orientations*. New York.

Könenkamp, Wolf-Dieter 1988: Natur und Nationalcharakter. Die Entwicklung der Ethnographie und die frühe Volkskunde. In: *Ethnologia Europaea* 18: 25–52.

Köstlin, Konrad 1994: Das ethnographische Paradigma und die Jahrhundertwenden. In: *Ethnologia Europaea* 24: 5–20.

Kretzenbacher, Leopold 1986: *Ethnologia Europaea. Studienwanderungen und Erlebnisse auf volkskundlicher Feldforschung im Alleingang*. Munich: Trofenik.

Lange, Charles 1970: European Ethnology and American Anthropology. In: *Ethnologia Europaea* 4: 5–8.

Lindner, Rolf 1989: Kulturelle Randseiter. Vom Fremdsein und Fremdwerden. In: *Kultur anthropologisch. Eine Festschrift für Ina-Maria Greverus*, ed. Chr. Giordano et al. Frankfurt, 15–28.

Löfgren, Orvar 1989: The Nationalization of Culture. In: *Ethnologia Europaea* 19: 5–24.

Lutz, Gerhard 1970: Deutsche Volkskunde und europäische Ethnologie. Zur Wissenschaftsgeschichte der 50er Jahre. In: *Ethnologia Europaea* 4: 26–32.

Lutz, Gerhard 1982: Die Entstehung der Ethnologie und das spätere Nebeneinander der Fächer Volkskunde und Völkerkunde in Deutschland. In: Nixdorf/Hauschild (eds.): *Europäische Ethnologie. Theorie und Methodendiskussion aus ethnologischer und volkskundlicher Sicht*.

Müller, Klaus E. 1973/74: Die Beziehung zwischen Subjekt und Objekt in der ethnologischen Erkenntnis. In: *Ethnologia Europaea* 7: 1–16.

Nixdorf, Heide, Thomas Hauschild (ed.) 1982: *Europäische Ethnologie. Theorie und Methodendiskussion aus ethnologischer und volkskundlicher Sicht*. Berlin: Reimer.

Niederer, Arnold 1970: Wege zum nationalen Selbstverständnis und zum Fremdverständnis. Einfühlung oder Empirie. In: *Ethnologia Europaea* 4: 43–49.

Niederer, Arnold 1976: Nonverbale Kommunikation. In: *Direkte Kommunikation und Massenkommunikation*, ed. H. Bausinger and E. Moser-Rath. Tübingen, 201–214.

Palairet, Michael 1987: The Migrant Workers of the Balkans and Their Villages (18th Century – World War II). In: *Handwerk in Mittel- und Südosteuropa*, ed. Klaus Roth. Munich, 23–46.

Picht, Robert 1987: Die "Kulturmauer" durchbrechen. Kulturelle Dimensionen politischer und wirtschaftlicher Zusammenarbeit in Europa. In: *Europa-Archiv* 10: 279–286.

Riehl, Wilhelm H. 1910: Die Volkskunde als Wissenschaft. In: *Kulturstudien aus drei Jahrhunderten.* Stuttgart, 195–218.

Rohan-Csermak, Geza de 1967: La notion de 'complexe ethnique européenne'. In: *Ethnologia Europaea* 1: 45–58.

Rohan-Csermak, Geza de 1967: Conférence internationale d'ethnologie européenne. Hässelby 1965. In: *Ethnologia Europaea* 1: 59–74.

Roth, Juliana 1992: Lernen für interkulturelle Kompetenz. In: *Grundlagen der Weiterbildung* 3,2: 109–111.

Roth, Juliana 1996: Interkulturelle Kommunikation als universitäres Lehrfach. Zu einem neuen Münchner Studiengang. In: *Mit der Differenz leben,* ed. K. Roth. Münster, 253–270.

Roth, Klaus 1988: Wie "europäisch" ist Südosteuropa? Zum Problem des kulturellen Wandels auf der Balkanhalbinsel. In: *Wandel der Volkskultur in Europa*. eds. N.-A. Bringéus et al. Münster, Bd. 1, 219–231.

Roth, Klaus 1993a: 'Interkulturelles Management' – ein volkskundliches Problem? Zur interkulturellen Dimension von Wirtschaftsunternehmen. In: *Der industrialisierte Mensch*, eds. M. Dauskardt and H. Gerndt. Hagen, 275–290.

Roth, Klaus and Gabriele Wolf 1993b: *South Slavic Folk Culture. Bibliography of Literature in English, German and French on Bosnien-Hercegovinian, Bulgarian, Macedonian, Montenegrin and Serbian Folk Culture.* Compiled and ed. by ... Columbus, Ohio: Slavica Publishers.

Roth, Klaus (ed.) 1995: Zeit, Geschichtlichkeit und Volkskultur im postsozialistischen Südosteuropa. In: *Zeitschrift für Balkanologie* 31: 31–45.

Roth, Klaus (ed). 1996: *Mit der Differenz leben. Europäische Ethnologie und Interkulturelle Kommunikation.* Münster, Munich: Waxmann (=Münchener Beiträge zur Interkulturellen Kommunikation, 1).

Samovar, Larry A., Richard E. Porter (ed.) 1991: *Intercultural Communication*. A Reader. 6th ed. Belmont, Cal.: Wadsworth Publ.

Schenk, Annemie und I. Weber-Kellermann 1973: *Interethnik und sozialer Wandel in einem mehrsprachigen Dorf des rumän. Banats*. Marburg.

Schenk, Annemie 1988: Interethnische Forschung. In: R.W. Brednich (ed.), *Grundriss der Volkskunde. Einführung in die Forschungsfelder der Europäischen Ethnologie*. Berlin: Riemer, 273–289.

Schier, Bruno 1966: *Hauslandschaften und Kulturbewegungen im östlichen Mitteleuropa*. Göttingen.

Schiffauer, Werner 1996: Die Angst vor der Differenz. Zu neuen Strömungen in der Kulturanthropologie. In: *Zeitschrift für Volkskunde* 92 (1996): 20–31.

Schuhladen, Hans 1994: Wieviel Vielfalt ertragen wir? Zur Pluralität der multikulturellen Gesellschaft. In: *Zeitschrift für Volkskunde* 90: 37–58.

Senghaas, D. 1982: *Von Europa lernen. Entwicklungsgeschichtliche Betrachtungen*. Frankfurt/M.

Stoklund, Bjarne 1972: Europäische Ethnologie zwischen Skylla und Charybdis. In: *Ethnologia Scandinavica*, 3–14.

Stoklund, Bjarne 1981: *Europäische Ethnologie*. Würzburg, München, 3–36 (= Ethnologia bavarica, vol. 9).

Svensson, Sigfrid 1973: *Einführung in die Europäische Ethnologie*. Meisenheim am Glan: Hain.

Szücs, Jenö 1990: *Die drei historischen Regionen Europas*. Frankfurt: Verlag Neue Kritik.

Theodoratus, Robert. J. 1982: The Contribution of American Cultural Anthropology to European Ethnology. In: Nixdorf/Hauschild, 145–163.

Trojan, Mieczyslaw 1983: Dreschflegel in Europa. Methodische Probleme einer Karte. In: *Ethnologia Europaea* 13: 203–226.

Tuomi-Nikula, Outi 1993: Stereotype und direkte Kommunikation. In: *Kieler Blätter für Volkskunde* 25: 89–110.

Viires, Ants 1977/78: A Proposition for the Typological Classification of European Farm Wagons. In: *Ethnologia Europaea* 10: 76–87.

Volbrachtová, Libuse 1988: Der Kulturschock der "kleinen Unterschiede". In: Ina-Maria Greverus et al. (ed.), *Kulturkontakt – Kulturkonflikt.* Frankfurt/M. Bd. 1: 209–218.

Watzlawick, Paul, Janet Beavin, Don Jackson 1967: *Pragmatics of Human Communication. A Study of Interactional Patterns, Pathologies, and Paradoxes*. New York: W.W. Norton.

Weber-Kellermann, Ingeborg 1967: Probleme interethnischer Forschungen in Südosteuropa. In: *Ethnologia Europaea* 1: 218–231.

Weber-Kellermann, Ingeborg, Andreas C. Bimmer 1985: *Einführung in die Volkskunde / Europäische Ethnologie*. Stuttgart: Metzler.

Weiss, Richard 1962: Die Brünig-Napf-Reuß-Linie als Kulturgrenze zwischen Ost- und Westschweiz auf volkskundlichen Karten. In: *Schweiz. Archiv für Volkskunde* 58: 201–231.

Wiegelmann, Günter, Matthias Zender, Gerhard Heilfurth 1977: *Volkskunde. Eine Einführung*. Berlin.

‘Killing the Dead’ in Šurmanci

About the Local Sources of ‘the War’ in Bosnia

Mart Bax

Bax, Mart 1996: ‘Killing the Dead’ in Šurmanci. About the Local Sources of ‘the War’ in Bosnia. – Ethnologia Europaea 26: 17–25.

Bosnia Hercegovina is the site of a striking number of Second World War monuments erected on or in the immediate vicinity of mass graves. Unlike war monuments and war graves elsewhere in Europe, these memorials are bones of contention and generate inter-ethnic violent animosity. This paper gives an extensive description of the trials and tribulations of one of these war monuments and the Serb and Croat communities involved. It addresses an aspect of ethnic cleansing that has hitherto been the focus of very little research, i.e. the destruction of mass graves. In addition, the paper advocates a more systematic inquiry into the local sources of “the war” in this part of the former Yugoslavia.

Prof.dr M.M.G. Bax, Professor of Political Anthropology, Department of Anthropology, Vrije Universiteit, De Boelelaan 1105, NL–1081 HV Amsterdam, The Netherlands.

“Far from simply serving to divert hostile impulses in a harmless direction, human ritual is employed to exhort people to war and violence – – – as long as intergroup hostilities have existed, rituals have been used to express them” (David Kertzer 1988).

“... the conditions that lead to (large-scale) violence require a micro foundation based upon social organization in rural and smalltown life ...” (David Laitin 1995).

“Bosnia-Hercegovina was a mass-murderers’ dream come true, a mighty necropolis of empty mass graves, high and dry, waiting to be filled” (Brian Hall 1994).

Introduction

Late in the summer of 1992, just before nightfall, a loud explosion resounded in Bijakovići. Bijakovići is one of the hamlets of Medjugorje, the parish in western Hercegovina that has expanded since the start of the alleged Marian apparitions there in the early eighties into a pilgrimage centre of world-wide importance (cf. Bax 1995). I was just about to get up from the table and see what happened when the huge hands of my host, Franjo B., pushed me back in my chair. ‘It is nothing ... we’ll stay inside’, he said emphatically. In bed that night, I thought it over. Apparently Franjo did not want me asking any questions. For that matter, no one of the family in the room had paid any attention to the explosion. It was as if everyone was prepared for it, and then simply went about their business.

We were working on the land the next morning when I brought it up again, but Franjo acted as if he did not hear me. It was not until the lunch break, when I said I would go have a look in the direction of Šurmanci, the hamlet I thought the sound of the explosion had come from, that my landlord and friend reacted. At the end of the afternoon, he said, he would show me what had happened.

Without a word, we drove toward Šurmanci in his old Volkswagen. I was familiar with the part of what barely deserved being called a road, for I had been there a year before ‘the war’. Since I was so insistent, my previous host and I were to visit a war monument. But before we had gotten very far, we were startled by a volley of rifle shots – coming according to my informant from *Četnik* sentinels – and we had no choice but to beat a hasty retreat.[1]

About half way, we turned into a side road. Unlike the first part, it was nice and smooth. We made another turn and a few kilometres further we stopped at what looked like a huge parking lot in the middle of nowhere. At the bottom of the ravine to the left, the Neretva River flowed past, and in the mountainside to the right steps had been hacked out leading to a shapeless mass of stone that lit up brightly in the setting sun. We silently climbed the partly ravaged staircase – sixty-eight steps, I remember. It stopped at a plateau with the remains of a monument. 'Comrades blew up this blasted *Četnik* thing', Franjo informed me with a torrent of curses. And in his school-English he added emotionally: 'We killed the dead because they kept them alive' – an ultimate form of ethnic cleansing, I thought.[2] He spit with contempt on the remains and turned away. He had barely given me time to film and to make pictures.[3] On our way back in the car, I felt the tension gather between us, and did not say a word. The road was so bad that the pipe of the cooling system of his old Polo broke, and when I started asking questions while he repaired it, that was when the 'bomb' burst. 'Why, why, why ... you always want to know why!' Hadn't I ever noticed that people didn't want to answer my questions about Šurmanci? (I had.) Hadn't I ever noticed that no taxi, or anyone at all, ever wanted to go to Šurmanci? (I had.) Hadn't I ever noticed that the people here all acted as if Šurmanci didn't exist? 'Look at the road. It is almost impossible to drive down that road. Everyone from around here tosses their garbage alongside the road. There are no signs telling you the way to Šurmanci. At the church, all the hamlets are listed on the big tablet – not Šurmanci. In all the guidebooks for tourists, the hamlets here are described – not Šurmanci. You can buy postcards and slides of almost every spot around here – not of Šurmanci'. Franjo concluded his tirade, alluding to my not being more perceptive, by saying: 'To us here, Šurmanci is dead ... we want to forget'.

A few days later, Father Leonard, one of the Franciscan parish priests, revealed a bit more of the secret. He told me people wanted to pretend Šurmanci did not exist because it reminded them of oppression, humiliation and forced labour. In the Second World War, he explained, many Serbs from the vicinity, especially from nearby Žitom, were killed by local *Ustaši*, as the Serbs invariably call the Croats, and tossed into the ravine at Šurmanci.[4] And since the establishment of the Communist Tito regime after the Second World War, their descendants and other relatives have been taking every opportunity to remind the Croats of what had happened. The monument at Šurmanci was the largest and most painful reminder. Father Leonard concluded: 'Here almost every village and neighbourhood has a painful reminder like that'.[5]

A few weeks later (I was gone by then), Medjugorje was startled by a few enormous explosions. Villagers from Žitom who were said to be fanatic Serbs had blown up the most crucial part of the bridge over the Neretva, destroying the most important connection between the Brotnjo Plateau and Mostar. Pursued by a group of Croat *rezervisti*, the people of Zitom fled with their families high into the Vjelez Mountains, where they settled in a former Muslim village now controlled by a Serb military unit.[6] At any rate for the time being, a long tradition of violence and enmity between two rural communities in the region had come to an end.

Since the outbreak of 'the war' in Bosnia Hercegovina in April 1992, a great deal of attention has been focused on what the underlying causes might have been. How is it possible, observers have wondered, that people who lived side by side in peace for decades on end suddenly developed such fierce animosity? The answer is often sought in the recent past: Tito's policy, aimed at the integration of Yugoslavia's many peoples and nationalities, failed; and the spectre of ethno-nationalism was revived (e.g. Glenny 1992, Slapšak 1993, Anstadt 1992, Irvine 1993, Pleština 1992, Schöpflin 1993, Brey 1993, Thompson 1992, Peternel 1993, Parin 1993 and Dringa 1993). Explanations of this kind certainly have their merits, but in one important respect they fail: they do not clarify why and how hostility between the ordinary people of rural Bosnia was perpetuated. Šurmanci's monument for the dead and the related enmity between the people of Medjugorje and Žitom provide an interesting opportunity to shed more light on this aspect. The case illustrates in detail that in actual fact this animosity never ceased to exist, but has been deliberately preserved and regularly nourished by collective rituals. For decades, the enmity was concealed by political terror and hidden behind the official communist rhetoric viewed in Western circles as the only truth. For a better understanding of 'the war' in Bosnia Hercegovina, more research is urgently called for at the local level and focused upon such ritual markers as war monuments cum mass graves.

Gatekeepers and Peasants

On the east bank of the Neretva River, where numerous roads lead from the mountain villages to the age-old trade route from Mostar to the Adriatic, there are a couple of small towns. These *vratari* (gatekeepers), as both the towns and their inhabitants are called locally, were founded in the early decades of domination by the Ottoman Empire, between 1470 and 1550. They were small garrison strongholds that oversaw the communication between the mountain villages and the market centres along the river. The predominantly Muslim population earned a living collecting the tributes for the various authorities, maintaining law and order in their area, and charging tolls on all the traffic of passengers, goods, and animals between the market centres and the peasant communities (Balić 1992, Vego 1981). In view of their functions, it is no wonder the gatekeepers were unpopular with the peasants and the merchants from the towns. They were regularly ambushed by gangs of revengeful peasants, who were just as regularly disciplined by the garrisons. Their wealth made the gatekeepers attractive to gangs of roving bandits (Koljević 1980, Balić 1992 and Wilson 1970).

Žitom was one of these gatekeepers; it controlled almost the entire Brotnjo Plateau. Žitom is still associated with a winepress (*presa za grozdje*), as the precious grape juice from the plateau was appropriated there, and the worthless peels remained behind.

When the Ottoman Empire began to waver in the latter part of the nineteenth century, a group of Serb rebels from Montenegro took advantage of the opportunity to conquer the rich town of Žitom, banish or murder the local population, and occupy the luxurious settlement themselves. However, the whole area soon fell under Hapsburg rule. In their efforts to pacify and incorporate the mainly Croat peasant population, the Hapsburgs were only too happy to use the militant Montenegrin Serbs (Soldo 1964, Vego 1981). For the Croats of the Brotnjo, ever since then Žitom has been a symbol of Serb oppression and exploitation.

In 1929, after the foundation of the Serb-dominated Kingdom of Yugoslavia, hostilities soon escalated and the region became the site of more and more bloodshed. Groups of East Bosnian *Četniks,* originally a loosely organized auxiliary of the national police, began to terrorize the population of the Brotnjo. With Žitom as their home base – and soon with the support of *mjesni četniči* (local fighters), they would pillage the plateau. They raped women, stole cattle, destroyed vineyards and water cisterns, burned houses and barns to the ground, and viciously penalized any resistance (Soldo n.d.). An elderly informant from Medjugorje, a twelve-year-old child at the time, compared those calamities to the recent hostilities: 'Nothing has really changed ... only the horses have become tanks and armoured cars'.

The officially authorized reign of terror of the *Četniks* evoked a Croat counterpart: supported by nationalistic political circles from Split and the surrounding area, Brotnjo peasants organized vigilante and resistance groups. Medjugorje became the centre of the new *Ustaša* movement for the Brotnjo, battling a perpetual 'mini-war' with Žitom (Soldo 1964, n.d.).

In the early years of the Second World War, this regional violence formation was incorporated into a war figuration of national proportions. Backed by the Axis powers, the Independent State of Croatia (NDH) was founded (1941), and Bosnia Hercegovina were to be part of it. With the help of the para-military *Ustaša* organization and not infrequently the overt support of Roman Catholic clergymen, the young state took every opportunity to cleanse Croatia and Bosnia Hercegovina of Serb elements. In addition to forced conversions to Roman Catholicism, mass deportations and massacres were among the means to that end (Alexander 1979, Ristić 1966, A. Djilas 1991, Maček 1957, Tomasevich 1975 and Jelić-Butić 1986).

In Medjugorje, the *Ustaša* headquarters of the Brotnjo, 'preparations were made for action'. Reportedly in conjunction with groups from Čapljina, Humac, and Široki Brijeg, plans were made to cleanse the peripheral regions of the Brotnjo. Žitom was high on the list in this connection. 'In the late summer of 1942, the time had come', one of my most belligerent informants told me. All the people of Žitom – in so far as they were not in active battle somewhere else – were taken prisoner and herded into a colossal bunker built into a cliff by the Germans. The plan to close off the entranceway and leave them there was abandoned, or so my informant told me, when a 'better' option came up. A column of lorries packed with Serb prisoners and led by Germans changed command near Žitom, and the Brotnjo *Ustaši* were now in control. They added their 'shipment' from Žitom and headed toward Šurmanci. There, far from the inhabited world, the prisoners were slaughtered like cattle and tossed into the ravine – nobody knows exactly how many.

Like the other hamlets involved in atrocities of this kind, Medjugorje was severely punished. In the end, the outcome of the reprisals, later carried out by Tito's Partizans, was that the parish of Medjugorje lost about half its population and suffered considerable material losses (Maček 1957, Craig 1988, Anonymous 1986).[7] This was not the end of it, for concealed behind official communist rhetoric, after the Second World War Medjugorje was to go through a lengthy period of subjugation and humiliation.

Forced Labour and Humiliation

The liberation committees set up by Tito and his Partizans in the Second World War to serve as local authorities in the conquered territories were not averse to the use of violence. In the post-war period as well, as the new 'civil society' was constructed, violence, intimidation and terror continued to be integral policy components (Alexander 1979 and Ristić 1966). Numerous newly created official positions on the federal, national and local levels were 'awarded' to 'liberators of the people'. Formally expected to carry out party politics, in actuality they ruled as potentates whose main aim was, to accumulate wealth and settle old accounts (Alexander 1979, Soldo n.d. and M. Djilas 1975).

Former Partizan commander Stojan Stojanović was the first to visit the ghost town of Žitom after the Second World War. Together with a few other young men who were members of the same clan, he had been able to escape the heinous revenge the *Ustaši* took on his native town. The men had joined a Montenegrin partisan unit. Their power and influence had mushroomed in the course of the post-war cleansing campaign in the region to eliminate the *Ustaša* movement. In view of their success, they were put in charge – allegedly by the party – of the administrative, economic and demographic reconstruction of Žitom.

Within little more than a decade, by the early sixties, it was as if a miracle had taken place in the ravaged town. Almost all the houses had been rebuilt and were now occupied by relatives of the former residents, the bridge over the Neretva had been repaired, the roads had been repaved, and a new small Serbian-Orthodox church had even been built.

Whence this 'miracle'? Some sources mention considerable sums of government funding supplemented by special Soviet aid earmarked for their sorely afflicted Serb brothers (Vego 1980, Soldo 1964). In another publication (Smilan 1977), references are made to continual assistance from Serb emigrants and *Gastarbeiter*. Still another source emphasizes the energy and the partisan mentality of the local population (Dragan 1978).

In addition to these possibly correct and relevant explanations, Soldo (n.d.) notes another point that deserves special attention here. After the Second World War, he observes, the Brotnjo – like other regions in Bosnia Hercegovina – was carved up into a number of unofficial provinces (*kolonije*) 'ruled' by (Serb) local partisan leaders: a power constellation that was still in existence at the outbreak of the most recent 'war'.[8]

Stojan Stojanović and his fellow clan members controlled Medjugorje and the adjacent neighbourhoods of Bijakovići and Šurmanci. The villagers have greatly contributed to the reconstruction of Žitom and the prosperity of its inhabitants. Up to the late sixties, every household that had been linked to the *Ustaša* movement (according to the authorities, that included all the Croat households in the region) had to make 'reparations' or pay off 'war debts' to the Partisan Fund, which was in actuality managed by the Serb establishment. Whoever refused to do so was accused of subversive nationalistic conduct, invariably resulting in imprisonment (Soldo n.d.).[9]

By the end of the sixties, these 'policies' made way in theory for a policy aimed at the promotion of 'brotherhood and unity', but in actuality served to reinforce ethnic animosity. The state government in Sarajevo made funds available to 'promote the cultural legacy', and local authorities could submit proposals in this connection.[10] In Medjugorje, the population was confronted with this 'promotion' in the spring of 1970. It took quite a bit of prodding on my part to get a few of the villagers to tell me about it. 'A van of armed men came: *Četniks* from (Žitom). They stopped at the crossing where the late Djure Šivrić's house used to be. Further down the road, they blocked off part of the mountain with little red flags ... Later we heard explosions, and that evening we saw part of the mountain had been blown up. Then we had to come and work, chopping stones and carrying them away. But no one came. That is why the police from Čitluk took the people from their homes. A lot of men fled to the mountains, but when they came back home at night, the police came and took them away'.

Bit by bit it became clear that the *Četniks* were building a monument for their Second World War comrades, and that the people from the Brotnjo (alleged *Ustaši*) had to do the actual work.[11] For almost three years, the people of Medjugorje, Bijakovići and Šurmanci did all they could to sabotage the work, but the authorities kept forcing them to do their share in building the monument. Without exception, obstruction led to arrests, which meant either paying a fine or doing a few days of forced labour.[12] Soon, the building site was popularly referred to as Goli Otok, after the notorious state prison off the Adriatic coast (Soldo n.d.).

After the unveiling ceremony on 27 April, 1973, the humiliation went on. The authorities never had trouble finding a reason to punish someone, especially considering the way the villagers were apt to act. Garbage discarded alongside the road had to be removed, potholes in the surface of the road had to be repaired, there had to be more and better parking space. There was an almost endless succession of sabotage and punishment, with annual peaks around 27 April. That was when thousands of detested *Četniks* would gather from far and wide in their automobiles to celebrate the past; Partisan heroism and party loyalty were the main themes on these occasions. They were loud-mouthed, or so I have been told, and uncouth, and this evoked local objections, which in turn incited the authorities to do their best to 'get matters back to normal', for example by ordering villagers to clean the streets.

Toward the mid-eighties, some years after the alleged Marian apparitions, which attracted masses of pilgrims, this complex of ethnic animosity, which was what it was, faded into the background. 'It was thanks to the power of the Mother of God', said Father Leonard, though others felt it was 'thanks to the economic boom in Medjugorje that the authorities benefited from as well'. Whatever the case may be, there were no further large-scale ceremonial events near the mass grave of Šurmanci.

In 1992, when the Serb-controlled state monopoly over the organized means of violence disintegrated, the monument near Šurmanci 'disintegrated' as well. 'But the memory lives on – on both sides', lamented the parish priest.

Conclusion

Šurmanci's monument for the dead is not the only one of its kind. Up to now (end of 1995), I have been able to trace sixteen similar 'ritual centres'. In all the cases, they are a symbolic expression of the long-term power and dependency relations between Serb power centres and the Croat communities dominated by them. And in all the cases, these emotionally charged sites were blown up by small militant groups of Croats shortly after the recent crumbling of the power apparatus, thus destroying the last territorial ties and claims of the opponent. The assumption would thus seem justified that there is evidence here of a more general pattern, characteristic of western and southern Hercegovina, of ethnically based antagonism between pairs or clusters of village communities.

If this assumption is founded, it can open new options for a better understanding of the recent 'war' in this part of the former Yugoslavia. It can then become clear that the bloodshed did not come out of the blue, nor was it the direct result of spectres that went back half a century and had mysteriously come to life again. Instead it constituted a temporary intensification and expansion of what is essentially an ongoing process of maintaining and reproducing extremely passionate antagonism between and sometimes even within certain ethnic groups, a process that mainly unfolds at a local level. It can also become clear that the term 'war' as it is used in Bosnia Hercegovina should not be taken to mean the same thing as in other parts of the world. The generic term *rat* not only pertains to violent processes between regular armies at the national level, but also to more private feuds between families and clans as well as all the more flexible and temporary violent operations at intermediary levels of social integration.

There is one question that should be addressed here: Why do Western circles know virtually nothing about this more general pattern of ethnically based antagonism? A partial explanation can be sought in the effective concealment strategies of the Communist regime under Tito. Every effort to draw public attention to nationalistic differences was relentlessly suppressed or depicted by the strictly censored Yugoslav state press as 'manipulation by capitalist powers', 'undermining activities on the part of subversive elements' or simply as the work of 'gangsters'. Virtually without a word of criticism, Western European intellectual and political circles accepted this version as the truth. Any critical inquiry into the recent past of Yugoslavia was punishable by a lengthy prison sentence (Balić 1992, Kideckel 1993 and Ramet 1984). In addition to Stalinist Communists, the infamous political prison at Goli Otok, situated near a popular tourist island in the Adriatic, was almost solely populated by historians, journalists, and authors who had shed a critical light on the former Yugoslavia's recent past (Balić 1992, Soldo n.d.).

This Western unawareness was not alleviated by any anthropological or ethnographic studies at the local level. On the contrary; in their impressive review article they wrote in 1983, Halpern and Kideckel did not mention a single publication about local-level political relations and processes, for the simple reason that there were none. The study of nationalism in Yugoslavia was taboo in anthropological circles, and that of ethnicity long remained confined to analyses of the cultural content of ethnic identity (e.g. Hammel 1969, Lockwood 1972, 1975, 1978, 1981) or focused on the politically relatively innocuous inter-state level (e.g. Beck and Cole 1981, Sugar 1980). And as late as 1991, in anthropological circles the phenomenon of ethno-nationalism in former Yugoslavia was dismissed as 'folk ideology' (cf. Šimić 1991). It was not until the recent outburst of violent warfare that anthropologists focused on the region became painfully aware of their selective attention and of its consequences for their perception of the local roots of 'the war' (e.g. Kideckel 1993, Halpern 1993, Šimić 1993, Denich 1991, 1993, Hayden 1993, Despalatović 1993, Ballinger 1994, Bowman 1994).

Norbert Elias repeatedly noted that social developments are characterized by a combination of regularity and randomness, explainability and pure chance. On lower levels of integration, occurrences that might be regular and explainable on a high level become erratic, upredictable, and dependent on random circumstances and personal quirks. Ever since the Middle Ages, the processes of state formation and state development in Western Europe have exhibited regularity and structure, development in a certain direction, and can be analyzed and interpreted as such (Elias 1982, 1989; see also Wilterdink 1993). It is from this perspective, characteristic of Western Europe, that the developments in former Yugoslavia in general and in Bosnia Hercegovina in particular are generally examined and evaluated, using terms like erratic, irrational, pointless and inconsistent. The case of Šurmanci shows that what might seem random and unpredictable on a higher societal level demonstrates a large extent of regularity and explainability at a local level. The conclusion seems obvious that for a better understanding of the recent problems in Bosnia Hercegovina – and possibly for the present problems of violence in Europe in general (cf. Laitin 1995) – attention should be more intensely and systematically devoted to processes and developments at lower levels of social integration.

Notes

* This article is based upon documents and field work I conducted intermittently between 1985 and 1995. The names of almost all the people and some of the places have been changed. I would like to express my gratitude to my informants in Bosnia Hercegovina and elsewhere in Europe for their assistance, protection and hospitality. For their comments on earlier versions of this article, I would like to thank Bill Christian, Ger Duijzings, the late Ernest Gellner, Caroline Hanken, Dieter Hanners, David Kertzer, Daan Meijers, Ed Koster, Estellie Smith, Lev Orec, Fred Spier, Sjef Vissers and Alex Weingrod. Of course I alone bear full responsibility for the contents of the article.

1. The term *Četniks* or *Četnici* originally referred to the legendary and often glamourized Serb buccaneers and gangs of bandits from the era of the Early Ottoman rule who, or so the story goes, rose up at regular intervals in an effort to cast off the despised Turkish yoke. In both of the world wars, *Četniks* were a para-military organization of Serbs who saw it as their formal task to support the regular Serb troops and maintain law and order in the region. In practice, however, it was not unusual for them to operate in small, independent units led by war lords and terrorize the Croatian and Bosnian Croat countryside. As such, they were extremely disliked by the Croat community. After the Second World War, these mini-armies soon fell into decline. Later, however, *Četnik* resistance groups were known to play an active role, especially in the eastern Bosnian countryside, where they were the 'strong arm' of regional ultra-nationalist Serb movements. Up to this very day, Croats and Muslims in Bosnia Hercegovina still call their Serb compatriots *Četniks*. For more information about *Četniks* past and present, see Čopić (1964), A. Djilas (1991), Tomasevich (1975) and Malcolm (1994).
2. In the Bosnian countryside, the deceased continue to be part of their kinship group. Via them, their progeny can lay claim to the use of land and water and to the produce of fruit and olive trees. It is not until all the traces of their lives have been wiped out that these claims cease to exist.
3. In the following year, after I had collected more extensive visual material about ravaged war monuments and mass graves, all that material that was so valuable to me was destroyed by a war lord from the vicinity. He had probably been informed about my activities, which might have compromised him. Using the threat of violence, he forced me to hand over my entire collection.
4. The *Ustaša* movement is also said to have originated in a distant past, when 'intrepid Croat warriors took arms against alien rule'. According to authoritative historical sources, however, the *Ustaša* movement emerged in response to the hegemonic aspirations of the Serbs in the first decades of the twentieth century. At the start of the forties, the movement became the official 'strong arm' of the fascist Independent State of Croatia (NDH). In fact, many of the units operated independently and cruelly terrorized the Serb people of Bosnia Hercegovina. After the Second World War, the movement was largely liquidated by the new Communist government. Nonetheless, a number of cells continued underground, especially in western Bosnia and Hercegovina, the birthplace and traditionally the centre of the movement. Up until today, Serbs from the region still call every Croat a *Ustaša* (plural: *Ustaši*). More information on this movement's past and present can be found in Jelić-Butić (1986), Ristić (1966), Banać (1984), Hory & Broszat (1965), Križman (1983), Starčević (1971) and Tomasevich (1975).
5. When the Communist regime in the former Yugoslavia began to disintegrate in 1982, people started to speak hesitantly and sometimes even to write about the Second World War mass graves and monuments and their background. Official, government-propagated views always seemed to have an unofficial counterpart sustained by the less powerful segment of the population, and diametrically opposed to the official version (cf. Glenny 1992, Brey 1993, Rathfelder 1992, Melčić 1991, Reissmüller 1992, 1993, Denich 1991 and Soldo n.d.). It nonetheless remained a highly sensitive subject, and when the 'big war' broke out in Bosnia Hercegovina in April 1992, the openness once again became a thing of the past.
6. *Režervisti* refers in popular usage to all the militias that were active in the recent 'war', including the independently operating war lords with their men as well as the reserve troops from the old state or federal army, the gangs of sol-

diers who had deserted and roved about the countryside plundering, and the 'weekend militias', which were bands of relatives and neighbours who went out to pillage and raid in hostile territory.

7. The partisans headed by Tito were the newest of the three 'resistance' movements active in Yugoslav territory during the Second World War. It was predominantly Serbs who joined this generally well-organized Communist military and political organization. Very few Croats from Bosnia Hercegovina played a role. After the war this organization was able to consolidate its power and establish a federation of socialist republics, initially following the Russian example. Almost all the important government positions were occupied by ex-partisans. Especially in Bosnia Hercegovina, it was not unusual for them to rule as local potentates. More extensive information can be found in A. Djilas (1991), M. Djilas (1975), Parin (1991), Maclean (1990), Roberts (1973) and Tomasevich (1975).
8. In 1992 I was informed about the existence of extensive documentation material on these ethnically based hostilities in the region. A reporter from *Mostarski List* had accumulated a collection of documents based upon his own investigations in the archives of the newspaper, awaiting an appropriate moment to publish them. I was able to read and leaf through some of them and make copies of certain parts I felt were extremely salient. When I wanted to continue my investigative work in 1993, the newspaper building turned out to have been completely destroyed, just as almost all the buildinqs in the centre of Mostar.
9. Almost all the young men of Medjugorje at the time spent time for this reason in the jails of Mostar, Sarajevo or some other town in the former republic of Bosnia Hercegovina.
10. Cf. *Mostarski List*, 12 March, 1968.
11. According to some sources, in the beginning of the sixties a modest monument had been built at the same spot. However, I was unable to uncover any further details.
12. Father Siro, who was serving the parish at the time, also had to haul stones as punishment for giving a sermon in which he compared the parishioners to the Jews who had to make tiles for the Egyptian oppressor.

References

Alexander, S. 1979: *Church and State in Yugoslavia since 1945.* Cambridge: Cambridge University Press.

Anonymus 1986: *Hercegovina u NOB-u(II)*, Sarajevo: Berdon.

Anstadt, M. 1992: *Al mijn vrienden zijn gek.* Den Haag: BZZToH.

Balić, A. 1992: *Das unbekannte Bosnien.* Wien: Böhlau.

Ballinger, P. 1994: The Politics of Submersion: History, Collective Memory, and Ethnic Group Boundaries, in: G. Bowman (ed.), *Antagonism and Identity in the National Idiom: The Case of Former Yugoslavia.* Oxford: Berg.

Banać, I. 1984: *The National Question in Yugoslavia: Origins, History, Politics.* Ithaca: Stale Press.

Bax, M. 1995: *Medjugorje; Religion, Politics, and Violence in Rural Bosnia.* Amsterdam: VU University Press.

Beck, S. & J. Cole (eds.) 1981: *Ethnicity and Nationalism in Southeastern Europe.* Amsterdam: Euromed Papers, No. 14.

Bowman, G. 1994: Constitutive Violence and Rhetorics of Identity: A Comparative Study of Nationalist Movements in the Israeli-Occupied Territories and Former Yugoslavia, In: B. Kapferer (ed.), *Nationalism and Violence.* Oxford: Oxford University Press.

Brey, T. 1993: *Die Logik des Wahnsinns. Jugoslawien – von Tätern und Opfern.* Freiburg: Herder.

Čopić, B. 1964: *Prolom.* Rijeka: Adria Press.

Craig, M. 1988: *Spark from Heaven.The Mystery of the Madonna of Medjugorje.* London: Hodder & Stoughton.

Denich, B. 1991: 'Unbury the Victims: Rival Exhumations and Nationalist Revivals in Yugoslavia', Paper: American Anthropological Association Annual Meeting, Chicago, pp. 1–14.

Denich, B. 1993: Unmaking Multi-Ethnicity in Yugoslavia: Metamorphosis Observed, *The Anthropology of East Europe Review (Special Issue)* Vol. 11 (1, 2): 43–54.

Dispalatović, E. 1993: Reflections on Croatia, 1960–1992. *The Anthropology of East Europe Review* 11 (1–2): 100–108.

Djilas, A. 1991: *The Contested Country: Yugoslav Unity and Communist Revolution, 1919–1953.* Cambridge, Mass.: Harvard University Press.

Djilas, M. 1975: *Wartime.* New York: Harcourt, Brace, Javanovich.

Dragan, V. 1978: *Žitomišlići – Istorija i Geographija.* Sarajevo: Muk.

Elias, N. 1982: *The Civilizing Process, Vol. II: State Formation and Civilization.* Oxford: Blackwell.

Elias, E. 1989: *Studien über die Deutschen.* Frankfurt am Main: Suhrkamp.

Glenny, M. 1992: *The Fall of Yugoslavia.* London: Penguin Books.

Hall, B. 1994: *The Impossible Country. Journey Through the Last Days of Yugoslavia.* New York: Penguin Books.

Halpern, J. 1993: Introduction. *The Anthropology of East Europe Review (Special Issue)* 11 (1–2): 5–14.

Halpern, J. and D. Kideckel 1983: Anthropology of Eastern Europe. *Annual Review of Anthropology* 12: 377–402.

Hammel, E. 1969: The 'Balkan' Peasant: A View from Serbia, In: P.K. Bock (ed.) *Peasants in the Modern World.* Albuquerque: University of New Mexico Press, pp. 75–98.

Hayden, R. 1993: The Triumph of Chauvinistic Nationalism in Yugoslavia: Bleak Implications for Anthropology. *The Anthropology of East Europe Review (Special Issue)* 11 (1–2): 63–69.

Hory, L. & M. Broszat 1965: *Der Kroatische Ustasha-Staat 1941–1945.* Stuttgart: Baum.

Irvine, J. 1993: *The Croat Question: Partisan Politics in the Formation of the Yugoslav Socialist State.* Boulder: Westview Press.

Jelić, I. 1978: *Hrvatska u ratu i revolućiji, 1941–1945.* Zagreb: Ziral.

Jelić-Butić, F. 1986: *Četnići u Hrvatskoj.* Zagreb: Ziral.

Kertzer, D. 1988: *Ritual, Politics and Power.* New Haven: Yale University Press.

Kideckel, D. 1993: Editor's Note. *The Anthropology of East Europe Review (Special Issue)* 11 (1–2): 3–5.

Koljević, S. 1980: *The Epic in the Making.* Oxford: Clarendon Press.

Križman, B. 1983: *Ustaše i treci Reich II.* Zagreb: Ziral.

Laitin, D. 1995: National Revivals and Violence. *European Journal of Sociology* 36 (1): 3–43.

Lockwood, W. 1972: Converts and Consanguinity: The Social Organization of Moslem Slavs in Western Bosnia. *Ethnology* 11: 55–79.

Lockwood, W. 1975: European Moslems: Ethnicity and Economy in Western Bosnia. *Anthropological Quarterly* 47: 253–269.

Lockwood, W. 1978: Social Status and Cultural Change in a Bosnian Moslem Village. *East European Quarterly* 9: 123–124.

Lockwood, W. 1981: Religion and Language as Criteria of Ethnic Identity: An Exploratory Comparison, In: S. Beck & J. Cole (eds.) *Ethnicity and Nationalism in Southeastern Europe.* Amsterdam: Euromed Papers, no. 14: 71–82.

Maček, V. 1957: *In the Struggle for Freedom.* Pittsburgh: Pennsylvania State University Press.

Malcolm, N. 1994: *Bosnia. A Short History.* London: Papermac.

Meštrović, S. 1993: *Habits of the Balkan Heart.* Houston: Texas A&M University Press.

Parin, P. 1991: *Es ist Krieg und wir gehen hin. Bei den jugoslawischen Partisanen.* Berlin: Rowohlt.

Parin, P. 1993: Woher dieser Hass? *Die Tageszeitung* (16-12-1993).

Paris, E. 1961: *Genocide in Satellite Croatia, 1941–1945: A Record of Racial and Religious Persecutions and Massacres.* (trs. Pois Perkins) Chicago: American Institute for Balkan Affairs.

Peternel, N. 1993: *Voorheen Joegoslavië. Achtergronden van de Balkanoorlog.* Amsterdam: Balans.

Pleština, D. 1992: *Regional Development in Communist Yugoslavia: Success, Failure and Consequences.* Boulder: Westview Press.

Rathfelder, E. 1992: *Krieg auf dem Balkan.* Hamburg: Rororo.

Reissmüller, J. 1992: *Der Krieg vor unserer Haustür.* Stuttgart: DVA.

Reissmüller, J. 1993: *Die bosnische Tragödie.* Stuttgart: DVA.

Ristić, D. 1966: Yugoslavia's Revolution of 1941. London: University Park Press.

Roberts, W. 1973: *Tito, Mihailovic, and the Allies.* New-Brunswick.

Schöpflin, G. 1993: *Politics in Eastern Europe.* Oxford: Blackwell.

Šimić, A. 1993: The First and Last Yugoslav: Some Thoughts on the Dissolution of a State. *The Anthropology of East Europe Review (Special Issue)* 11 (1–2): 14–21.

Slapšak, S. 1993: *Joegoslavië, weet je nog.* Amsterdam: Mets.

Smilan, I. 1977: *Dokumenti.* Sarajevo: Muk.

Soldo, J. 1964: *Čitluk i Brotnjo: Istorija.* Zagreb: Privredni Vjesnik.

Soldo, J. (n.d.) *Mali rat u Brotnju.* (manuscript).

Stanojević, B. 1989: *Crvena Gospa iz Medjugorja.* Beograd: Panpublik.

Starčević, A. 1971: *Politicki i spisi.* Zagreb: Ziral.

Sugar, P. 1980: *Ethnic Diversity and Conflict in Eastern Europe.* Santa Barbara: ABC-Clio.

Tolstoy, N. 1986: *The Minister and the Massacres.* London: Century Hutchinson.

Thompson, M. 1992: *A Paper House: The Ending of Yugoslavia.* London: Vintage.

Tomasevich, J. 1975: *The Chetniks.* Stanford: Stanford University Press.

Vego, M. 1981: Historija Brotnja. Čitluk: Svjetlost.

Wilson, D. 1970: *The Life and Times of Vuk Stafanovic Karadzic 1787–1864.* Oxford: Clarendon Press.

Wilterdink, N. 1993: Staatvorming in figuratie-sociologisch perspectief. *Antropologische Verkenningen* 12 (4): 59–71.

When Pilgrims Emigrate

The Skaro Pilgrimage to Our Lady

Henriette A. Kelker and David J. Goa

Kelker, Henriette A. and Goa, David J. 1996: When Pilgrims Emigrate. The Skaro Pilgrimage to Our Lady. – Ethnologia Europaea 26: 27–35.

Polish immigrants in Alberta, Canada, have, since their arrival 100 years ago, established shrines and initiated pilgrimages as a way to re-establish a cultural and religious rhythm which had been temporarily interrupted by their journey. In this paper, the pilgrimage to the Lourdes Grotto at Skaro, Alberta, is explored against the background of the Polish immigrant history in Alberta, and of a changing pilgrimage tradition in the Western world. The phases of pilgrimage as discussed by Victor and Edith Turner are also the key phases of immigration. While its old heritage anchors the Albertan pilgrimage firmly in the European tradition, the immigrant journey which is shared by the Polish pilgrims adds a dimension to the Albertan pilgrimage which is uniquely Canadian.

Henriette A. Kelker, Research Associate, Provincial Museum of Alberta, 12845 - 102 Avenue, Edmonton, Alberta T5N 0M6, Canada

David J. Goa, Curator of Folklife, Provincial Museum of Alberta and Adjunct Professor, St. Stephen's College, University of Alberta, 12845 - 102 Avenue, Edmonton, Alberta T5N 0M6, Canada. E-mail: DGoa@mcd.gov.ab.ca.

"Whan Zephirus eek with his sweete breeth
Inspired hath in every holt and heeth
The tendre croppes, and the yonge sonne
Hath in the Ram his halve cours yronne,
And smale foweles maken melodye,
That slepen al the nyght with open ye
(So priketh hem nature in hir corages);
Thanne longen folk to goon on pilgrimages..."
(The Canterbury Tales)

Immigrants bring with them to Canada a living tradition, a cultural memory and their own ways of satisfying their daily needs. Domestic crafts, culinary specialties, celebrations, and worship patterns are all part of this wealth of skills and knowledge. In the Polish community, initiating pilgrimage was a way to re-establish a cultural and religious rhythm which had been temporarily interrupted by immigration. However, there are now many annual pilgrimages to shrines erected by pious Catholics who sought this particular kind of religious experience. In Alberta, where the first Protestant clergy arrived only 155 years ago, and the first Catholic priest four years later, Christian pilgrimage can hardly be called a tradition. But the increasing popularity of pilgrimage in Alberta stems from motivations and experiences which are markedly different from those contributing to recent increases in popularity of pilgrimages in Europe.

The development of pilgrimage in Alberta raises a number of interesting cultural anthropology and social history questions. To consider these questions, first we will place the Polish-Canadian community's pilgrimage to the Lourdes Grotto at Skaro against an historical background of both pilgrimage in general and the pilgrimage tradition in Poland. Second, we will consider the Skaro pilgrimage in the context both of the Polish immigrant community in Alberta and of a changing pilgrimage tradition in the Western world. Third, we will review the process of pilgrimage and discuss the similarity between the process of pilgrimage and the process of immigration. Fourth, we will examine the pilgrimage to Skaro in terms of its function within the Polish-Canadian community. Both the contextual description as well as the functional analysis are based on interviews with immigrants conducted during 1994 and 1995, as well as on the scholarship about immigrant and religious history in this province.

Prior to World War I many Polish immigrants were motivated to come to Canada by extreme poverty at home and by an abundance of cheap land in Western Canada. The Honourable Clifford Sifton, Canada's Minister of the Interior, promoted Eastern European immigration in order to develop Western Canada. While many in Poland were poor, only those in the provinces which were part of the Austro-Hungarian Empire were free to emigrate. From 1895 to 1914, farmers from Galicia settled in the rural areas around Edmonton. At the same time, mining companies in Alberta recruited skilled labour from Silesia. Thus, Southern Alberta received many Polish people from this region. After World War I, although many still came from poor rural areas, increasing political tension became a major motive for immigration.

The Polish-Albertan pioneer period has been extensively documented by Joanna Matejko in her collection of interviews and memoirs of Polish settlers in Alberta (Matejko 1979). The early immigrants worked as farm labourers (Edmonton area), in logging camps, in mines (Banff, Crowsnest Pass, Drumheller), and on the railway (Calgary). The recorded stories speak of a life of determined hard work, isolation, and the building of close communities.

After World War II, immigrants came to Canada to build a new life free from the communist government. Veterans, survivors from concentration camps, military prisoners, and displaced persons arrived after several years of travel, battle, and detainment. During the 1960s and 1970s Polish people continued to come to Canada to seek freedom from communism. Many were accomplished scientists, whose professional opportunities were limited in their own country. Some were sponsored by relatives who had settled in Canada in a previous generation, which explains why extended families with similar regional backgrounds tend to live in the same areas of Alberta.

A dramatic increase in immigration occurred in the 1980s when Poland came under martial law. Between 1985 and 1994, a total of 3,500 immigrants were sponsored by the Immigration Commissions of the respective branches of the Canadian Polish Congress in Calgary and Edmonton, Alberta's two major cities of around 500,000 inhabitants each.

While life in the early part of the century was hard, it was characterized by an elemental simplicity. Immigrants built up a new life literally with their own hands. Many who have arrived here more recently experience greater difficulties adapting, because of a different social infrastructure, political system, and work condition.

Polish identity is marked by a deep Marian devotion, a rootedness in the land, and a history of war, oppression, and boundary changes. "Matka Boska" is celebrated as the patron saint of seeding and planting, hay-making, and harvest (Przybylski 1966), while as "Queen of Poland" she has inspired the Polish nation during centuries of battle, as well as during its proud intellectual and artistic development. The life of the Virgin Mary moves through the life of the Polish people and orients them in time and place. People participate in pilgrimage because it is time to do so. The liturgical calendar is part of the popular and local spiritual rhythm which announces pilgrimages as regularly as it announces summer and winter. Resistance to social reorganization by the communists was effectively accomplished through reinforcement of the established patterns of the Church and the rhythms of popular piety. Communal participation in pilgrimage throughout the year is one significant place where religious and national consciousness reinforce each other. The congruence of ecclesiastical forms and popular piety sustained in many a deep sense of patriotism and expressed the unity of the Church and the Polish people (Piwowarski 1982).

Popular piety in many countries of the world has remained stubbornly unmoved at times of sweeping social and political change, offering the community the power to prevail and the courage to resist. Religious rites in general, and pilgrimage in particular, gained significance in Poland after World War II. Because "Poles had

Fig. 1. Building the grotto in 1918: a community effort. Courtesy of the Provincial Archives of Alberta.

no state of their own, they identified themselves with Catholicism, which not just guarantees identity, but also protects human dignity and hope" (Piwowarski 1982: 26).

Polish immigrants coming to Alberta at different times have all had to reorient themselves physically and spiritually in a new world. Few images connected them with the familiar environment they had left, and no received local tradition embodied the rhythm of life. The religious expression of the Polish community, both the language of gesture and the use of the mother tongue, made the church a particular cultural landscape largely separate from the public sphere of the local community. The need for priests knowledgable of the customs of the different immigrant groups is well illustrated by an anecdote related by Fr. Anthony Sylla, a priest who served the Polish community in its initial settlement:

"When Easter came, the pioneers, (not having a priest of their own) brought food to be blessed to St. Mary's church, as was customary with the Poles and Ukrainians. Father Lacombe, who was then the parish priest, thought that the good people were bringing presents to him. He asked the lay brothers to gather all the food and bring it to the rectory. But the 'good' people refused to give the food and tried to explain, as well as they could, that they wanted it blessed. Father Lacombe was only too happy to bless it ..." (paraphrased, Matejko 1979: 350–351).[1]

Polish settlers started coming to Alberta in 1895. During the first years of settlement, the immigrants were occasionally visited by the

Fathers Wolciech and Kulawy from the Holy Ghost Parish in Winnipeg, over 1000 km away. In 1889, the diocese of St. Albert attracted Father François Olszewski to serve the new immigrants. Soon after his arrival the diocese secured land to build the first chapels in Skaro and Krakow, both about 100 km East of Edmonton. As more Polish people came into the province, the blessing of newly completed churches in the area around Edmonton came to be an annual occurrence. Many rural communities had built churches before Poles began settling in cities. The first Polish church in Edmonton was built in 1913.

In the summer of 1918, Father Antoni Sylla, omi, took the initiative to build a grotto at Skaro in east central Alberta named for the pilgrimage of Lourdes. Father Sylla was born in Popielów, Poland, in 1881, but left Poland as a young boy in search for work. At the age of 14 he chose to become a priest and received his education from the Oblate Fathers in Valkenburg and in Houthem, the Netherlands, and in Hünfeld, Germany. It is probably during these years that Fr. Sylla became acquainted with the many Lourdes Grottos built of rocks and cinders that were popular in the Western European mining districts. These shrines provided the model for the grottos he built in several Polish-Canadian communities on the prairies, where the local farmers gathered rocks as they cleared and prepared fields for cultivation. There was plenty of this hard won building material.

By local account it took 600 wagon loads and 300 bags of cement to build the Skaro grotto. The first pilgrimage took place on August 14, 1919, two months after placement of the first stone. Today, more than 75 years later, between 3,000 and 5,000 people come from all over Canada to its annual pilgrimage on the Feast of the Assumption of the Virgin Mary, which begins on the eve of August 14 and moves through the feast day on the 15th.

The shrine was built on donated land next to the church. This process of choosing a pilgrimage site was remarkably pragmatic compared to the apparitions and miracles which inspired many of the European pilgrimage sites.[2] This comparison does not faze Polish immigrants. As one informant pointed out: "Divine power manifests itself in curious ways and the act of offering land may well be as much inspired by divine will as is the recognition of the Virgin Mary standing on a rock. After all, who selected Mount Sinai as a place for revelation — Moses or Yahweh?"[3] What matters is that the annual pilgrimage to Skaro shapes an annual journey to a sacred place, to visit historically significant ground, and to participate with thousands of others in worship.

John Huculak, the grandson of the donors of the Skaro grounds, wrote of the events preceding the building of the shrine (Huculak 1990). Huculak notes that an influenza epidemic struck the community in 1918, the same year in which the new Skaro church was dedicated to the Assumption of the Holy Virgin on August 14. Over 1,000 people attended this dedication – a huge number at a time in which church dedications were a common occurrence. No doubt such a crisis, to say nothing of the shadow of the Great War and the advent of Bolshevism, galvanized the Polish community. Against this historical backdrop, the Polish community re-created its pilgrimage tradition, a means of participating in the rhythm of life and death which had been established by their ancestors in the old country. After this unexpectedly large gathering at Skaro, the decision was made to build a shrine.

The shrine of Our Lady of Lourdes at Skaro is closely associated with the cemetery, and no pilgrim fails to pay a visit there during their pilgrimage. The monument to the Pioneers, located at the edge of the cemetary, reads: "In remembrance of our pioneers, who built our first church in the year 1900." The community actively maintains the connection with the first pioneers. School children in the Polish programs learn about their pioneer history and about Skaro. The pictures drawn by students from the Polish program at St. Basil's school in Edmonton, after their pilgrimage to Skaro, give remarkable prominence to the cemetery. During discussion, too, students commented repeatedly on the prayers at the cemetery for the repose of the souls of the people buried there. Here they encountered the names and burial spots of many young children and thus contemplate human mortality.[4]

The Skaro pilgrimage today draws people from Alberta and beyond. The numbers of pilgrims have varied over the years, with a marked increase in the past decade. Some of the increase can be attributed to the increased Polish population in the province. Since Father Strankowski became parish priest of Skaro in 1986, his publicity program also invites non-Polish churches in the Calgary and Edmonton dioceses to the annual event. In 1993 the Skaro church celebrated its 75th anniversary, which created some additional interest, and in the past two years, the date of the pilgrimage has fallen on the weekend, enabling greater numbers of pilgrims to attend. In 1995, the 100th anniversary of Polish settlement in the province has been celebrated with a year of extensive festivities, culminating in the pilgrimage attended by Archbishop Szczepan Wesoly from Rome. The Archbishop is a delegate of the primate, Cardinal Glemp, and is appointed by the Vatican to look after the spiritual needs of Polish priests serving the diaspora Polish communities. There were over 4,000 pilgrims in 1995.

Pilgrims come by bus, car, or camper. The pilgrimage stretches over two days and families engage old friends, touch ancestral ties in the cemetery and in the telling and re-telling of local story, and, cultivate their faith through the various liturgies. The pilgrims' journey includes the gathering of the community, praying the rosary in Polish and English, a vesper service in Polish, confession, and then Divine Liturgy in the evening. A few hardy pilgrims park in the nearby town of Star and walk the last 10 km to the grotto. For those who come by bus, the opportunity to sing Marian hymns during the ride prepares them for the evening. Priests from the region hear numerous confessions at the *prie-dieus* which are discretely placed in the woods surrounding the site. The market atmosphere of pilgrimages has a modest expression at Skaro with a few stands where the faithful may purchase books, religious objects, candles, and food to augment their picnic baskets. The colour guard of the Knights of Columbus[5], the procession, and the Liturgy — normally, celebrated by the Archbishop of Edmonton — builds up to the climax of the pilgrimage. At dusk the pilgrims carry candles and form a procession along the main pathway of the grotto. The procession moves slowly as the faithful sing hymns to Our Lady. Many pilgrims stop along the pathway and pray at one of the statues. Some leave their candles at various places along the way, stuck on rocks and ledges all around the grotto. More candles are carried to the cemetery where soon the whole grave site is alight. This procession captures the heart of the Skaro pilgrimage. Its power lies in the people's ownership of the celebration.

The Marian aspect of many pilgrimages in Europe has been re-oriented at Skaro. The presence of the Archbishop for the Liturgy on the eve of the Feast of the Assumption of the Virgin Mary highlights a particular challenge Roman Catholicism faces in the Alberta context. The local diocese has a number of churches which retain their ethnic character, although it is clear from various Canadian Catholic documents that this is simply to accommodate the large immigrant populations until they acculturate to Canada.

Rome has long been uneasy with churches that are an intense part of the cultural and national life of a people, particularly where ethnic Catholics are in the minority. The Ultramontanism debates of past centuries remain in the background of the Skaro pilgrimage but it is noticeable in the theme the Archbishop commonly addresses in his homilies. Over a number of years the Archbishop has used this occasion to temper the faithful's devotion to the Virgin Mary, pointing out that, as much as she is to be loved, she is not the focus of the spiritual life of Roman Catholics. Rather, they must remain vigilant to ensure that the Holy Trinity is always the focus of their piety. They may appreciate the Virgin Mary but must never let her impede their focus on Christ and the Holy Trinity. What is worthy of note here is that, within the context of this feast dedicated to the Virgin, the Archbishop has moved from building his homily on her place in the spirituality of Poles, to orienting the spiritual focus away from this dimension of popular piety. In a diocese where a Polish church is something of an anomaly accommodated for historical reasons, the pilgrimage dedicated to Mary, at her pilgrimage

Fig. 2: The Skaro Grotto ready for the Feast of the Assumption of Our Lady, August 14, 1995. Courtesy of the Provincial Museum of Alberta.

site, and with considerable cultural memory associated with such a focus, is treated with a touch of uneasiness by the Archbishop. In a Polish cultural context, it is difficult to imagine a priest or bishop not using the opportunity to emphasize that dimension of the spiritual life of which Mary is the symbol and focus.

Europe has witnessed a significant increase in the popularity of pilgrimage during the past decades. Not only has the number of pilgrims climbed to new heights, but the age profile of participants has changed. The tourist industry has been quick to develop pilgrim tours, souvenirs, literature, and audio-video products. The "motivation clusters" driving the modern pilgrimage are complex and must be seen as a system of interacting forces, none of which is solely responsible, and all of which are affected by each other (Post: 1989). Renewed interest in participation parallels a growing interest in spectatorship. At the local level, in many cases, one can speak of the "staging" of a pilgrimage to which both participants and spectators flock in droves, as they do to a variety of historic re-enactments (Post 1991). This is not to say that there is not also a certain renewal of religious piety at the same time, especially among young people. As one participant on the pilgrimage to Czestochowa observed: "Quand j'étais jeune prêtre, je me rappelle que les fidèles avaient peur de parler de Dieu. Ce n'est plus le cas aujourd'hui..." (Giovannoni, Mallein & Szot 1990: 51).

Media coverage plays a major role in developing people's awareness of spectacular events. The media have long been reporting on the major pilgrimage sites in Europe, and have increasingly focused the public eye on the smaller local events by listing them in calendars of attractions, encouraging tourists to seek these events out as a destination for their outings. The tourist industry is both pro-active and reactive in this. It actively promotes its own interest and creates a market for itself, while responding to perceived trends and developing interests.[6]

In Alberta there is no question of any tourist industry promoting pilgrimage, or of the accommodation of spectators. The Skaro setting is remote and rural, in an area where farms are five to ten km apart. The closest town of a few hundred inhabitants is Star, 10 km south and the closest point of recreational interest, Elk Island National park, is 20 km south. The pilgrimage to Skaro is known only among Poles and those who live in the immediate vicinity. "Sightseeing" is not yet a motive for participation. Yet every year more people converge at this sacred site. The word is spreading among Roman Catholics of non-Polish origin and the number of Poles who attend is continuing to rise.

The increased popularity of pilgrimage in Europe has sparked a new, or renewed, interest in pilgrimage as a cultural and social phenomenon. In a clearly organised overview of themes and trends in pilgrimage research since 1986, Paul Post shows the impact of an increasingly interdisciplinary approach in developing a new understanding of pilgrimage in a varied contextual structure (Post 1994). The analysis of motives for some European pilgrimages is relevant to research on Canadian pilgrimage because it illuminates the complexity of the motivation clusters and the interaction of various social and religious factors. The immigrant history of Western Canada introduces a number of new factors to be explored in relation to pilgrimage.

Although the functions of pilgrimage are many, its process is characteristic and holds a degree of constancy through the ages. Victor and Edith Turner's division of the pilgrimage process into the three phases of detachment, liminality, and transformation, continues to be a valuable analytical theory. The Turners' model is based on van Gennep's analysis (Van Gennep 1908). According to van Gennep, rites of passage ritualise the experiences characteristic of the passage from one phase of life into the next and enable the community to participate in this otherwise private development. The process of passage resembles the process of immigration. The journey into the unknown is a recurring theme in both Hebrew and Christian scriptures, from the departure of Abraham and Sarah from Ur to the journey of the Apostle Paul among the gentiles. This journey, undertaken to satisfy a need for a closer encounter with God, is a search for fulfilment.

The phases of pilgrimage as explained by the Turners – the death of the old which occurs when one embarks on a pilgrimage, the period of unstructured potential in which *communitas* occurs as a gift of grace, and the transformation marked by re-entry into a structured life at a new level – are likewise the key phases of immigration. For the immigrant, the irrevocable loss of homeland remains a haunting occurrence throughout life. Hence the prominent role of the pioneer cemetery, where not just the bodies of loved ones are buried, but where a reminder of the lost past with which one continues to feel close ties remains.

The phase of liminality, or unstructured openness to possibilities, is particularly significant in immigration. Virtually no situation the new immigrant faces has routine answers and solutions. The future unfolds at the margin of the past which has been left behind, without the interference or guidance of an established pattern. At this threshold, unburdened by the expectations of convention, the immigrant has little choice but to interact fully with the opportunities offered by the future. Because this unstructured state (at least at the level of self-understanding) is by nature unstable, few people remain comfortable there for very long. Yet in this phase human potential for creativity is often realised and the personal accounts of the early pioneers reflect this. Matejko has recorded many examples of the resourcefulness and creativity displayed by new immigrants (Matejko: 1979). In this phase, also, both isolation and *communitas* are most strongly experienced.

Emigration is a journey toward a new life in a new land. The realization of this goal is marked by the appropriation of new ground as "one's own". Emigration is also a journey toward the re-creation of a structured life. Structure emerges through the integration of the new physical surroundings with a continuing cultural memory. This takes time as the emerging pattern needs to be both functional and comfortable, providing cultural identity as well as room to be alive in a new world.

Apart from the experiences of individual immigrants, the immigrant community as a whole can be seen as having moved through the rites of passage process. When considering the history of pilgrimage in Poland and the settlement history of the Polish immigrants sketched here, it is clear how the two processes resonate when superimposed on each other. Initially there was no Polish community in Alberta, merely clusters of individual immigrants in a new land. Eventually local communities were forged, finding their identity in a common heritage and shared experience. In order for pilgrimage to serve the same function for immigrants in Canada as it does for people in Poland — integrating the rhythm of worship with the rhythm of life — it is necessary for the immigrants to have reached a stage of stability. Thus the people need to have discovered a new rhythm in their lives which includes moments for acknowledging gifts, for grieving losses, and for experiencing a closeness to the new land. By 1918, the Polish community had come to such a stable stage in its life. They had a new homeland and a new community. The newcomers had established themselves on land they could call their own and together they had encountered many crises. To give expression to feelings of grief as well as thanksgiving, the community needed to add a new dimension to its worship.

Father Sylla sensed the longing and the readiness of the community to establish a pilgrimage through which the people could express all the grief and joy of their new life in a new land. The building of the shrine at Skaro has its roots in the Polish folk tradition, according to which pilgrimage is part of the rhythm of life. At the end of the pilgrim's journey the celebration of the Mass completes the re-entry into the structured world. For the Polish settlers, the first pilgrimage to Skaro completed a journey and acknowledged re-entry into a world which they now knew was their own. This process of revalorization is an annual experience at the Feast of the Assumption of the Holy Virgin. For the immigrant pilgrim, the encounter with the familiar symbolism of the Roman Liturgy becomes a moment of being part of the new world and of the kingdom of heaven, of coming home and of facing the world anew.

The pilgrimage to Skaro, since it is barely seventy-five years old, has a particular place among pilgrimages. Few communities today combine such a short history with such an old heritage. The short history makes the observation of its development unusually accessible, while its old heritage anchors the pilgrimage firmly in the European tradition. Against the backdrop of a complex system of influences, the pilgrimage to Skaro emerges as a dynamic event which continues to develop. During the 1980s, when Polish immigration to Alberta reached new heights, so did the pilgrimage to Skaro. This increase in enthusiasm still continues. Since the lifting of martial law in Poland, Polish immigrants often travel to Europe to participate in pilgrimages in their home country and other places. These travellers return with renewed zeal and bring back some of the European revival ethos. However, while the pilgrimage to Skaro may reflect some of the renewed popularity of European pilgrimages, it remains closely linked to the immigrant history of the pilgrims, thus adding a dimension to its function which is uniquely Canadian.

Notes

1. Father Albert Lacombe (1827–1916), an Oblate priest, is one of Western Canada's most famous missionaries. He devoted most of his life to work with the Cree and Blackfoot peoples and on occasion served Polish and other settlement communitites.
2. Turner & Turner point out that "Whereas medieval Marian pilgrimages are seldom known to have begun as the immediate consequence of a vision, the post industrial pilgrimages clearly owe their origin to particular visionary or apparition experiences." The origin of the medieval pilgrimages is seldom identifiable, their "foundation narratives have a mythical quality and seem to have arisen long after the pilgrimages were operant" (Turner & Turner 1978: 209).
3. Interview with a pilgrim from the Edmonton Polish community.
4. Taped interview. Provinvial Museum of Alberta, Folklife Collection. tape # AU95.9
5. The Knights of Columbus, a fraternal and beneficent society of Catholic men, was founded in New Haven, Connecticut in 1882. It is a popular society in Canada and is devoted to Catholic education

and charity. They characteristically provide a uniformed honour guard at the Skaro pilgrimage.

6. Similar developments have been noted in Japan, where a renewed interest in pilgrimage has been accompanied with materialistically oriented marketing techniques, advertising, air-conditioned busses, and luxury hotels for pilgrims (Reader 1987).

References

Barber, Richard W. 1991: *Pilgrimages.* Woodbridge.

Delameau, Jean 1986: Official and Popular Religion in France during the Reformation and Counter-Reformation. In: *Concilium* 186: 12–19.

Dussel, Enrique 1986: Popular Religion as Oppression and Liberation: Hypotheses on its Past and its Present in Latin America. In: *Concilium* 186: 82–94.

Giovannoni, François, & Vianney Mallein & Jerzy Szot 1990: *Czestochowa, l'espoir s'appelle Marie.* Paris.

Huculak, John 1990: *History of the Shrine Parish.* Edmonton.

Mach, Zdislaw 1992: Continuity and Change in Political Ritual: May Day in Poland. In: Jeremy Boissevain (ed.): *Revitalizing European Rituals.* New York: 43–61.

Matejko, Joanna 1979: *Polish Settlers in Alberta: Reminiscences and Biographies.* Toronto.

Monter, William 1983: *Ritual Myth and Magic in Early Modern Europe.* Brighton.

Parker, Cristian 1986: Popular Religion as Protest against Oppression: The Chilean Example. In: *Concilium* 186: 28–35.

Pieper, J., & P. Post & M. van Uden 1990: Beweegredenen. Sociaal-wetenschappelijke peilingen naar bedevaart motieven. In: *Volkskundig Bulletin* 16: 176–202.

Piwowarski, Wladyslaw 1982: The Problem of the Folk Church in Poland. In: *Concilium* 154: 12–20.

Piwowarski, Wladyslaw 1986: The Guarantor of National Identity: Polish Catholicism. In: *Concilium* 186: 20–27.

Post, Paul G. J. 1988: Onderweg, Tussentijdse notities met betrekking tot bedevaart onderzoek. In M. van Uden & P. Post (eds.): *Christelijke bedevaarten.* Nijmegen: 1–38.

Post, Paul G. J. 1989: Bedevaart zonder Grenzen. In: *Tijdschrift voor Liturgie:* 135–156.

Post, Paul G. J. 1991: Het verleden in het spel? Volksreligieuse rituelen tussen cultus en cultuur. In: *Jaarboek voor Liturgie-onderzoek:* 79–121.

Post, Paul G. J. 1994: Thema's, theorieën en trends in bedevaart onderzoek. In: J. Pieper, P. Post, & M. van Uden (eds.): *Bedevaart en pelgrimage: Tussen traditie en moderniteit.* Baarn.

Przybylski O.P., Bernard 1966: Our Lady and Poland. In: *The Immaculate* 17.3: 41–42.

Reader, Ian 1987: Back to the Future: Images of Nostalgia and Renewal in a Japanese Religious Context. In: *Japanese Journal of Religious Studies:* 287–303.

Sumption, Jonathan 1975: *Pilgrimage: An Image of Medieval Religion.* Totowa, NJ.

Turner, Victor 1969: *The Ritual Process.* Chicago.

Turner, Victor, & Edith Turner 1978: *Image and Pilgrimage in Christian Culture.* New York.

Van Gennep, Arnold 1960 (1908): *The Rites of Passage.* London.

Creating Life and Exploring Death

Susanne Lundin and Lynn Åkesson

Lundin, Susanne and Åkesson, Lynn 1996: Creating Life and Exploring Death. – Ethnologia Europaea 26: 37–49.

In Sweden, as elsewhere, people's lives and physical bodies have become part of an advanced medical care apparatus. The present article is about this technologization of everyday life and the integration of medical high technology in the biological process. The empirical foundation is the creation of life with the aid of *artificial reproduction* and the investigation of dead human bodies for the purposes of *autopsy* and *transplantation*. Life and death are undeniably two focal points where the encounter of medicine, biology, and culture is made visible. By looking closely at the techniques that make it possible to stretch these fundamental principles, we want to reason about changes in people's cultural identity.[1]

Susanne Lundin, Ph. D., Research Fellow, and Lynn Åkesson, Ph. D., Research Fellow, Department of European Ethnology, University of Lund, Finngatan 10, S–223 62 Lund, Sweden. E-mail: Lynn.Akesson@etn.lu.se.

Life and death, when they are problematized, are seen to have many features in common, revealing several general associations. Both *in vitro* fertilization and the encounter with death raise a number of existential questions. Life and death are self-evident opposites, yet each presupposes the other. It is difficult to reflect about death without simultaneously wondering about the meaning of life. When questions like these are raised, we also see clearly the ambivalence that people experience when life and death are explored. What is right or wrong is not given once and for all but is negotiable in any particular situation. This highlights the relation between biology and culture. How far can and should one reshape biological givens to achieve culturally desirable goals? Where is the limit to what is humanly irreplaceable?[2]

In this context one can ask what it means that we today not only use our physical appearance as an instrument for communication, but that it is also possible to change and reshape our bodies as we please (Mestrovic 1993). Now women without fallopian tubes can give birth to children, infertile men can become fathers, and seriously ill or dying people can be granted new life through organ donation. The artificial fertilization of eggs, and the combination of different persons' bodies through organ transplants, or even the practice of injecting the brain substance of aborted foetuses into people suffering from Parkinson's disease – such techniques undoubtedly indicate that our bodies are replaceable. At the same time, they blur the distinction between life and death.

Empirical material concerning life and death will be used here as a basis for our contribution to an ongoing discussion in cultural theory. This has increasingly focused on the interaction of societal structures, identity, and body. The aim is to discern how general processes and cultural patterns can be manifested in the individual's body (cf. Foucault 1991 [1963]; Giddens 1993; Melucci 1992). The modern Swedish society of the early twentieth century is a good example of such links. People were given everything from rational infant care at the start of life to concerned nursing in late old age. This revealed the plan economy not only of the state but also of the body; the citizens' bodies became important cogs in a general *collective* machinery (Frykman 1994b).

In today's post-modern society we see a different linkage between individual and society. There is much to suggest that we are living in an age that is obsessed, more than ever before, with *individual identity*, and where it is not primarily collective but personal needs that are signalled through our bodies.

In what follows we want to test these perspectives by drawing attention to specifically Swedish experiences of artificial reproduction, commonly known as test-tube babies, and the handling of dead bodies. First Susanne Lundin looks at the problematic of *in vitro* fertilization, under the heading "Creating Life". Then, with a corpse on an autopsy table as a starting point, Lynn Åkesson goes on to reason about "Exploring Death".

Creating Life

There are some questions that always have a capacity to stir up people's minds. One of these is undoubtedly the question of what is naturally and genuinely human. With today's technology we can transgress old boundaries, namely, those surrounding our biological bodies. People's thoughts about biology and advanced medical methods are therefore a rewarding approach to a cultural analysis that seeks to arrive at a knowledge of the cultural principles underlying the ethical standards of modern society. We have seen a number of fruitful attempts to reveal our norm systems (Rapp 1993; cf. Strathern 1993a, 1993b). Far fewer studies, however, focus on the question of how people in their everyday lives handle experiences of living in a high-tech biomedical society. The aim of this discussion is therefore to acquaint the reader with some people who have a close concrete relationship to high technology. They are Swedish couples who are unable to have children and who therefore try to become parents with the aid of assisted conception.

The interviews conducted with these couples are permeated with a great ambivalence suggesting that both the original childlessness and the technologization of reproduction arouse complex feelings. The ambivalence is exacerbated by the fact that the dividing lines between natural and unnatural show such large national and cultural variations. In Sweden, for example, there is a special linkage between the view of nature and the view of humanity which is probably of significance for both state practice and popular ethics.

My informants' reflections about involuntary childlessness and artificial reproduction provide an empirical gateway to the subject. The focus is on the relation of individual needs and strategies to the cultural framework of society: how the biological urge to have children interacts with the more socially formed dream of parenthood.

Life Outside the Body

When I interviewed the first couple I expected them to be reticent. I thought that I would have to coax them to talk about a sensitive and tricky subject. It turned out instead that they spoke both willingly and eloquently about their lives. It is possible that thoughts about reproduction and its conditions open people's minds to a multitude of existential questions. Most of the interviewed couples, regardless of their origin and education, showed precisely this kind of self-reflexivity and capacity to regard society critically.

One of the couples, Eva and Lars, were for many years among the 10–15 per cent of the Swedish population who are unable to have children. I met them just after they had been through their sixth attempt at artificial insemination, the *in vitro* fertilization that led, after five years of repeated treatment, to a child.[3]

It was in 1988 that Eva was informed that her fallopian tubes were blocked and that she could not become pregnant naturally. Not content with this, the couple decided to try to become parents with the aid of technology.

The aspiration to have children is, of course, not unique to our own times. Even if the reasons have varied – everything from children as a guarantee of the survival of the collective to today's view of the family as an individual emotional project – infertility in itself has always given rise to elaborate programmes of action (cf. Sachs 1993). We find everything from religious blessings and folk cures such as scattering quick-growing peas in the bed,[4] to the biomedical and genetic techniques of the late twentieth century.

It is good to bear in mind the deep historical roots of this search for suitable measures to cure infertility when we discuss today's view of how we can deal with involuntary childlessness. Artificial fertilization has been transformed in just a few years from science fiction into a part of everyday life for many people. The first so-called test-tube baby was born in England in 1978 (Brinsden & Rainsbury 1992). The method has quickly spread all over the world, which means that childless women today can choose *in vitro* fertilization, with the ovum and the sperm uniting in the test-tube to create new life outside the body.[5]

In our modern society, then, we do not have to content ourselves with bygone ritual practices; medical intervention can correct our physical defects (cf. Melucci 1992:120). Today we have the potential to change, create, and recreate what is ostensibly biologically determined (cf. Featherstone 1992; Frykman 1994). This potential is naturally a source of joy to many people; it gives a cure to those who are barren and childless. However, if we listen to the voices that can be heard in literature, film, theatre, and art, we are also made aware of a serious threat. The overarching problematic concerns what is ethically defensible and biologically negotiable (Arditti, Klein & Minden 1984).

The Technologization of the "Natural"

In May 1993, Eva was wheeled into the operation theatre of the women's clinic. She was groggy from the tranquillizers and needed help from the anaesthetist to get into the gynaecologist's chair. The doctor inserted the ultrasound probe in Eva's body. The screen showed the fallopian tubes and the ovaries with the follicles hovering like balloons. They were the target for the doctor, who punctured the follicles with a thin needle which also caught the ova. A while later, the ova were put in a nutrient solution to be united soon after with the husband's sperm. It was here, in the laboratory, that the seeds of human life began to grow.

Eva and her husband Lars were already back home at the moment when the fertilization took place. While their ova and sperm were being cultured, they waited in suspense for a message from the hospital that everything had gone well and that the ova were ready to be implanted in the womb.

A short time after, the signal came. Eva once again got into the gynaecologist's chair and the fertilized eggs were carefully inserted in her uterus.[6] While the operation was in progress, Lars sat in the waiting room. A few minutes later, Eva came out, pregnant.[7]

Eva's pregnancy thus began with an operation that was not very different from a normal gynaecological examination. All this may seem far removed from what we normally associate with the conception of a child, but nevertheless a handy method for treating childlessness. Artificial fertilization, however, is not simple or something to be taken for granted; nor is it painless.

For Eva the way to a child was a long one; after several years of medical treatment, repeated attempts at insemination, miscarriages, and mental ups and downs, she gave birth to a son. Over these years she had acquired a very different attitude to herself as a woman, to thoughts of family and kin, as well as to her own body. Reproduction, which is regarded as the most natural thing in life by many people, became for Eva and Lars a highly mechanical and at times even artificial process. The young woman gradually came to view her own body as a machine, an object which, with the aid of advanced technology, could be a potential carrier of a future child.[8]

There is undoubtedly a great deal to suggest that a change occurs in our perception of reality and the self when technology intervenes in the domains of the body, when we realize that sexuality can be replaced by medical skills and that biological limits can be stretched, for example, by making infertile men into fathers and women with defective fallopian tubes into mothers (cf. Assier-Andrieu 1994; Giddens 1993).

But it was not just this changed self-understanding, a sort of physical and mental integration with technology, that Eva went through. Her view of the boundary between natural and unnatural was also affected. Above all during many of the unsuccessful attempts at fertilization, she was burdened by thoughts about how far man can intervene in what appears to be given by nature. The failure to become pregnant became for her a sign that someone, a divine force or the power of nature, wanted to punish her. But she was also haunted by anxiety about what the result of artificial fertilization could be. She often wondered *what* would come out of her body. What if someone had manipulated the ova? Thoughts like these continued to disturb her even after the child was born. Her dread of "reprisals" was expressed in fears that the child might not be her own: perhaps other ova and sperm had been substituted by mistake.

Eva's fears about what happens when technology intervenes in the human body resemble the message of books and films from *Frankenstein* to *Terminator* and *Jurassic Park*. They also remind us of today's headlines in the media, where there are debates about whether it is ethically defensible to transplant the ovaries of dead girl foetuses into infertile women, or to use technology to blur the boundary between life and death (cf. Lundin & Åkesson 1994). We also hear stories about Swedish women in their sixties who go to clinics in Italy to become first-time mothers through ovum donation, or about infertile women who become pregnant with the aid of ova from their own mothers.

Such reports can shake our view of the family and raise the spectre of incest, especially if insemination is done, for example, with sperm donated by the woman's own father. Is it possible, in other words, for genes to commit incest (cf. Edwards 1993)? In Sweden there are far more restrictions on *in vitro* fertilization than in many other countries (SOU 1985, 1989). The Swedish laws thus make the culturally formed question about incest via genes into a hypothetical question, but such questions are posed in both the international and the Swedish debate and are transformed in Sweden, with the help of the media, into a real threat.

Parallel to the ardent desire to have children, then, many people wonder whether biomedical solutions are morally acceptable. In Sweden it is considered unethical, for example, to be able to choose the sex of the child, as people can do in some private clinics in England.[9] Equally unacceptable are the solutions practised in India, where there are commercially operated clinics offering abortions to women if antenatal diagnostics show that the child is a girl. Some of my informants even wonder whether Sweden might see the growth of a black medical market for sorting out unwanted hereditary characteristics.

An Authentic Family

Despite such fears, many couples go abroad to have children in a way that is considered unethical in Sweden. The issue bears thinking about: what is it that creates such *ambivalence* about how to handle the possibilities offered by medicine? Perhaps it is the case that coping with childlessness actually takes place at the intersection between optimism about the future and a kind of cultural insecurity (cf. Ziehe 1989). As Alberto Melucci argues, people have a sense of bewilderment when offered ultramodern technologies to restore what is "natural" and give birth to children; a situation like this highlights many of our fundamental values about what is genuinely and irreplaceably human (cf. Melucci 1992; Kemp 1991).

The actions of my informants, however, should not just be seen as an encounter with the culturally unknown, but also as a confrontation with what is established and normal. In most societies, being a parent is regarded as self-evident, while childlessness is a departure from this normality. In Sweden, moreover, perhaps more so than in other western cultures, the view of a well-functioning society has long been associated with ideas of a limited family: mother, father, child.[10] Although this pattern is changing today as a result of divorce and remarriage, leading to new siblings and new parents, and also as a result of the adoption of children from other countries, the idea of the "natural" biological nuclear family still survives.[11] These ideas are reflected, for example, in Swedish legislation.[12] Ovum donation is prohibited in Sweden, which means that only the biological mother is permitted to give birth. The same view of genetic closeness and the demand to be able to trace one's own genetic origin can be seen in the Swedish laws on sperm donation. The anonymity of donors is not protected, as it is in most other countries; a child resulting from artificial insemination by a donor is entitled to be informed of the identity of his "real" father.[13] In modern Swedish society, then, ideas about reproduction and parenthood seem to be associated with the idea of what I would call *close genetic bonds of kinship.*

Among the nearly nine million people who live in Sweden, there are at least 250,000 couples who cannot become parents, who cannot fit the picture of a society where the biological family is taken for granted as the nucleus.[14] Many of them struggle with delicate questions about authenticity, about gender identity and parental identity. Not only do they have to renounce a biological yearning, they also feel a sense of social alienation. Longing for children is certainly a matter of needs and drives, but it is also a desire for social community.

That is why the encounter with "ordinary families" provokes strong feelings in many childless families and also raises a number of questions about the construction of the self in relation to other people. Or, as one informant said, "One wants to be normal, to have children the way other people do." Eva tells how, when she was childless, she increasingly avoided contact with friends and acquaintances who had children. When she met a pregnant woman or a pram on the street, she felt that her own stomach was unbearably flat and that her breasts had dried up; it was as if her body had come to symbolize and even proclaim her infertility and estrangement (cf. Wirtberg 1992).

Many of the interviewed women refused to accept the life offered them by their bodies. Several of them claimed that their real self was a fertile mother figure while their physical body was a sort of enemy: a stranger who had to be overcome in order to create a whole individual. By being pregnant and having a new-born baby, they longed to manifest the identity concealed in their body.[15] It almost appears as if the cultural reality for these women was felt to be stronger than the biological reality, and that these ideas about authenticity required an adjustment of the biology.

Biology and Culture

The birth of children is a biological fact. Through reproduction people become visible as biological creatures with drives, instincts, and feelings (cf. Haraway 1992; Mestrovic 1993). But these basic physical phenomena contain more than just data on menstrual cycles and hormonal changes; these processes are also formulated in cultural terms so that we can handle them. Fertilization and childbirth are revealed and confirmed in social patterns such as parenthood and family structure.

It is within this framework, which we may call the biocultural context, that my informants express their anxiety about the consequences of artificial reproduction while simultaneously refusing to accept their childlessness. Their reflections are based on a clear biological disposition but are shaped by a specific conceptual model. Their thoughts express the cultural contradiction that permeates western society. The idea of eternal naturalness – inviolable nature and human matter protected against intervention – is closely interwoven with our contemporary desire to reshape the world to suit our own needs.[16]

It is in the intersection between these different conceptual models that many people try to conquer parenthood; modern techniques make it possible to maintain traditional ideas about gender identity, family, and kinship. In this way the new technology allows not only biological but also social and cultural reproduction. This will to influence – even to correct – what appears to be determined by fate reflects a modern attitude. In this context, *in vitro* fertilization appears like a melting pot, where the rationality of the technological age meets our deep-seated ideas about what is biologically determined and universally human.

Exploring Death

The body of the dead woman on the autopsy table is still whole and almost unreal in its reality. It is difficult for an unaccustomed observer to separate the person who once lived from the matter that now constitutes nothing more nor less than a dead body. The face is covered, but the hands are expressive, fine-boned, beautiful, frozen in position, with a light-coloured band on the ring finger of the left hand, where the wedding ring was once worn. One arm is raised slightly in a gesture that invites many possible interpretations. A strange silence prevails in the brightly illuminated autopsy room of the institute of forensic medicine in Lund. There is a striking contrast between the dead body for whom time has stood still, and the cycling students outside the window on this warm April day when nature is turning green. It is the contrast between life and death, between movement and total stillness.

But the dead body has a story to tell. It will soon be opened. The organs will be removed and penetrated in a set order. This is done objectively, efficiently, and professionally. The cause of death will be established to give comfort to the bereaved relatives, to aid the growth of medical knowledge, and to satisfy society's need to guarantee the rule of law.

The woman who once was, who left her family in the prime of life, aged 55, caused imbalance and confusion by her death, leaving many questions unanswered. Some of them will be answered by the autopsy. Some of the imbalance that arises when a living body is transformed into dead matter will be redressed. Through order and strict medical classification, the balance will be restored: this and only this has happened to the body. It can give a sense of security to know the true cause of death.

The confrontation with a dead person arouses many existential questions, as it has done all through history. The questions can concern the potential danger of the deceased, the insight into the fragility of one's own life, or the close link between life and death. Almost inevitably there is the question of what happens to the self, the identity, the soul, when the body dies.

These are the themes that interweave and overlap in the following reflections. My interest is focused on the dead body.[17]

The Ambivalent Corpse

The danger of a dead body is evident from records in the Swedish folklife archives from the late nineteenth and early twentieth centuries. Both historical and contemporary examples in ethnological and anthropological literature testify to the same danger (e.g. Hagberg 1937; Bloch & Parry 1982). Countless precautions have been taken to protect the living from the destructive powers of the dead. It is only after a scrupulously observed and correctly performed burial ritual that the status of the dead person as really dead is confirmed. A dead but unburied person is in a transitional state or a cultural no man's land, and situations like this are, as we know, always charged with danger and ambivalence (cf. Douglas 1979; Turner 1985).

The power of the dead person is not only destructive. It can also be utilized to cure disease or to aid reproduction. Bones from dead people or soil from a cemetery could give good growth in the fields, successful fishing, plenty of milk, or good beer (Hagberg 1937:636ff.). Ideas that the fertile or reproductive powers of the dead can be transferred in symbolic form not just to fields and livestock but directly to human reproduction are described in an anthropological anthology showing how the theme of fertility is part of the actual burial ritual and the handling of the dead body (Bloch & Parry 1982).

This theme is not as evident in Sweden, but we can nevertheless detect a similar association between death and reproduction, such as the custom of dressing the corpse in a bridal shirt or shift, or dressing the corpses of young girls in full bridal attire; or the fact that the woman who washed the body was sometimes the same person as the midwife (Hagberg 1937:127, 177, 181, 194). Another fascinating theme is that women in their capacity as life-giving mothers are also thought to be closest to death. Bloch and Parry (1982:21) present a variety of anthropological examples to illustrate the links between femininity, sexuality, corruption, death, the body, and flesh, in contrast to the association of masculinity with fertility, the grave, and bones. The Aztec myth about Coatlicue, the life-giving and death-bringing goddess who is "tomb and womb at the same time" is another example (Gonzales-Crussi 1993:58). The topicality of the theme in the modern western world can be illustrated by the fascination with the mixture of (female) sexuality and death in popular fiction. Robert Tracy, for example, sheds light on this with the aid of the vampire genre in his essay "Loving You All Ways: Vamps, Vampires, Necrophiles and Necrofilles in Nineteenth-Century Fiction" (1990).

This ambivalent attitude to dead people, like the notions of links between female sexuality and death, is a good illustration of the interweaving of biology and culture (cf. Rosenbeck 1989:44). Being born and dying can appear to be purely biological facts. Ideas that a corpse can threaten or cure, or that women are closer to death, can appear to be nothing more than cultural constructions. Yet cultural constructions are, in the first place, just as real and concrete as biology. Secondly, there are no objective biological criteria for when life either begins or ends. Opponents of abortion, for example, differ from pro-abortionists in their view of when life begins. In the same way the criteria for death vary according to whether death is related to the activity of the brain, the heart, or the lungs.

Life through Death

Conceptions about the association of reproduction and death perhaps express a fundamental human idea that people must die so that others may live. We all have to make way for our descendants in an eternal cycle.

This general idea about the dead making way for or giving strength and life to the living and the as yet unborn, however, has acquired a new meaning through modern transplant technology. As we saw above in the section "The Technologization of the 'Natural'", it is medically possible that an ovary from a dead woman can once again be fertile in a living body through transplantation. While the old body is decomposing and disappearing, its reproductive capacity could live on in a new body. This is still not permitted, but other parts of the body are considered to be replaceable, and a dead person's organs can allow someone else to go on living.

But how far should we go? When does a person cease to be the same person? How many spare parts from other people or from dead people can we receive without losing our authenticity? These problematic and controversial issues raise the question of the boundary between life and death in a new form.

The problem is brought to a head in the case of pregnant women who are brain-dead. The record for a woman in this state functioning as a living incubator is 108 days. "Who is to decide in such cases?" wondered a doctor who cited the example with concern; the husband, the woman's parents, the doctor? Who is to say when the respirator should be switched off?

Transplants presuppose brain death, a death criteria introduced in Sweden in 1988 (SOU 1989:99, p. 13). There is a great demand for organs and a shortage of donors. This state of affairs nourishes the modern legend tradition which Bengt af Klintberg sums up in the complex of motifs entitled "The Stolen Kidney". These legends are about how unsuspecting people become the victims of veritable organ gangs (af Klintberg 1994; Moravec 1993). The theme is naturally used in films and novels too. The issues of "spare-part man", genetic manipulation, and life created outside the body are likewise gratefully exploited for films and popular fiction. As so often, art and the legend tradition seize on and give form to our existential fears. It is surely no chance that every self-respecting detective film nowadays contains detailed scenes of post mortems, or that the role of the forensic pathologist is given more and more space (cf. Saynor in *The Observer* 19/12 1993). Another example is the American photographer Andres Serrano's suites of pictures from the morgue, where the observer is confronted with embodied death in an eerie, frozen, timeless moment (Serrano 1993). Just like the body of the dead woman on the autopsy table, they lead our thoughts to life, to the incomprehensible similarity of the dead to those who are still alive.

The Authentic Body

It can naturally be argued that we have now distanced ourselves so far from death and the everyday handling of dead bodies that we are fascinated by it;[18] the repression of death is supposed to create a seed-bed for fascination with it. There may be some truth in this claim, but a changed perception of the body, that is, conceptions of what the body represents, is at least as important an angle for understanding modern man's horrified fascination with dead bodies. This modern ambivalence is not of the same kind as that expressed in the historical and anthropological examples. It is scarcely the danger or wholesome powers of the corpse that people are now revolted or attracted by. It is rather the dead body in its identity-bearing capacity that we relate to.

The link between body and identity offers an interesting way of interpreting the increasingly elaborate autopsy scenes in detective dramas. The observer sees or comes staggeringly close to the total destruction of the self. At the same time, reconstruction brings order, clarifying the course of events that preceded death. In this way, the post mortem represents both a terrifying dissection and a fascinating restoration of personal identity.

If the body has become an increasingly significant bearer and expression of personal identity (as maintained by scholars such as Featherstone 1992; Giddens 1993; Melucci 1992), the death of the body becomes the death of identity. To put it another way: if one no longer makes a distinction between body and soul, the flesh that was once regarded as merely the earthly shackles of the immortal soul now actually becomes one with the soul. When viewed in this light, the hesitancy of relatives to allow organ donations becomes comprehensible. It expresses a desire to preserve as a whole what once constituted the self. A dead body is unable to restore its authenticity and genuineness. It is up to the living person to constantly recreate himself.

Receiving organs does not upset this process of recreation. Nor does organ donation, as long as the donor himself has made the decision. Self-determination and hence responsibility with respect to one's own body is a characteristic of modern man. Authorizing interventions in another person's body, on the other hand, is problematic, since it can be seen as a violation of the other person's integrity and right to self-determination. The body as a sphere of personal responsibility applies to the dead as well.

The belief in the integrity and inviolability of the dead body also permeates the view that has been launched in recent government commissions of inquiry in this field, especially in the report on "The Body after Death" (SOU 1992:16). There is constant stress on the importance of handling dead bodies in an ethically correct manner, showing the same respect and consideration as we do to a living body. No operations apart from very minor ones may be undertaken without the consent of the relatives. The view of the commission of inquiry can be briefly summed up as follows: the dignity of the intact body and the influence of the relatives takes precedence over the need for medical knowledge. The frequency of autopsies, which was once very high in Sweden by international standards, has fallen by 30 per cent, and it is suggested that it should be further reduced.[19] The justification cited is not primarily economic (changed priorities in medical care) but ethical.

The stress on the intrinsic value of the dead body and its equality to living bodies is not a matter of course. Behind the commission's way of reasoning we detect a changed view of the body. Interestingly, it is closer to the layman's view of the body than to the view held by medical experts.

In medicine in general and forensic medicine in particular, staff have an everyday familiarity with the fragility of the human body. The wholeness and permanence that we fondly ascribe to it are in fact of short duration. People whose routine work involves handling dead bodies naturally make a sharp distinction between living and dead, associating the soul or the self with living persons only. For the rest of us, it can be difficult to dissociate the person from the body. Psychologists speak of a "lingering illusion", that is, that we attribute properties to the dead body which only a living person can have (Sanner, SOU 1989:99, pp. 81 ff.).

Forensic doctors are fully aware of this. They know what the appearance of the dead body means to the relatives, which means that they abstain as much as possible from any interventions which can disfigure the body once the autopsy is complete. In other words, theirs is a very correct and real construction of the human body. And it does occur that relatives actually check that the body has been neatly sewn up under the shroud. The relative wants to be sure for one last time that the integrity of the defenceless body has been restored. With the organs put back in the skilfully sewn up corpse, the person is preserved as he or she once was, as whole, genuine, and authentic as ever.

Laymen throughout history have also been eager to ensure that the dead body is kept intact. Otherwise the ghost could return to the living, demanding the missing part of the body, or even a lock of hair that someone cut off as a keepsake.[20] The dangerous powers of the dead person must also have been an active obstacle to all kinds of disfigurement of the dead body. Theologians dismissed these notions as primitive superstition, but the Christian belief in resurrection undoubtedly encouraged them. The idea that the soul would be reunited with a new bodily form, not of flesh and blood, in the life beyond the grave was – and is – on a relatively high level of abstraction. The theological view of the unimportance of the physical body was presumably not shared by people in general. But the reasons were different from what they are today.

The report on "The Body after Death" contains a brief survey of the attitude of different religions to interventions in the dead body. It declares that opposition to autopsies and the like rarely receives theological support, at least not in the Christian tradition (SOU 1992:16, pp. 71f., 353ff.).[21] And even though ideas of Christian origin have remained a part of our conceptual patterns in a secularized world (cf. Åkesson 1991:160), the most important dividing line between experts and laymen today is scarcely that between the priest and his congregation. It is more likely the dividing line between doctor and patient (cf. Frykman 1981; Lasch 1977).[22]

But the medical hegemony over our bodies has also been questioned. One expression of this is in the flourishing alternative therapies and health movements (cf. Frykman 1994; Lundin 1987; Salomonsson 1987). Heightened demands for the personal right to the body are also seen in the case of the dead. Until just a few years ago this was a medical or a state concern, but now relatives are entitled to see dead bodies at the institute of forensic medicine. We can draw parallels to the stillborn children that mothers were never allowed to see a few years ago. Now it is instead considered important for the parents to be together with the dead child. At the University Hospital in Lund these small creatures are photographed, nicely dressed and arranged, for the benefit of the parents. After an interlude of some fifty years, we are now seeing a return to the custom of wanting to see the corpse, at least among the immediate family. From the decades around the turn of the century there are plenty of pictures of dead children (but not of stillborn babies) in the Scandinavian archives (Kildegaard 1985).

This new-fangled return to something that feels historically familiar is due the realization by health service personnel that social death is necessary for the mourning process. To be able to mourn for someone, to understand death, an authentic body is needed. The fact that a government commission presenting a report like "The Body after Death" has come close to the layman's perspective, sometimes in opposition to the wishes of medical science, is probably an expression of this insight.[23]

Body and Identity

Artificial reproduction and the handling of dead bodies give us important information about the interaction between societal structures, identity, and the body. They also tell us something about the extent to which it is collective or personal needs that are signalled via the body. On the basis of the two empirical fields studied here, we think that we can say that the experience of living in a high-tech society, where questions of life and death have become negotiable, means a changed identity perception, a different view of the self. There appears to have been a shift of periphery and centre; the centre of people's consciousness is no longer society as much as the self.

This does not mean, however, that people's bodies have ceased to be an expression of collective needs. There is rather an interaction between social structure and the satisfaction of personal needs.

As regards the dead body, the interest in preserving the body intact and authentic testifies to the strong bond between identity and the body. This individual need for wholeness can be stretched, however, as the positive Swedish attitude to autopsies shows. Swedes are willing to place corpses at the disposal of science for the collective good. After the autopsy the wholeness of the body can be restored, which means that individual and collective needs do not need to conflict.

In this respect, artificial reproduction is more problematic. Having a child by *in vitro* fertilization satisfies personal needs of both a biological and a collective kind. But these personal needs have an age limit in Sweden. Collective needs define a "natural" family. In this family there is no room for, say, women who become pregnant after the menopause. There is no mistaking the significance of the fertile or infertile body for identity. Here people are prepared to adjust biological conditions which run counter to their view of the right cultural identity.

People's reflections about life and death have been among the eternal and existential questions throughout history. This means that the view of life and death includes both topical comments on today's society and ideas with deep historical roots. This combination of topicality and history makes issues of life and death into rewarding focuses for anyone seeking to understand how individual needs relate to the societal framework, and how this relationship changes through time.

Translation: Alan Crozier

Notes

1. The present work is part of a research project entitled "Transformations of the Body", in progress at the Department of European Ethnology, Lund University. See e.g. Frykman 1994a. Questions about life and death, along with other critical processes in the course of human life, such as puberty and ageing, is examined in greater detail in the anthology *Kroppens tid* (The Time of the Body), ed. Susanne Lundin and Lynn Åkesson, 1996.
2. "The irreplaceable" is the title in translation of Peter Kemp's book about how people live in relation to high technology, how people in everyday life deal with ethical questions associated with, for example, biomedicine (Kemp 1991).
3. My studies of artificial reproduction are largely based on interviews with childless couples and health service staff. The informants' descriptions of childlessness and their attempts to remedy this have provided valuable material to supplement historical, statistical, and medical data.
4. The Swedish folklife archives have records of many folk narratives and practices about remedies for childlessness.
5. The first test-tube baby in Sweden was born in 1982. Today there are between one and two thousand Swedish children born by this method.
6. In Sweden the doctors have a policy of reducing the number of implanted ova, since, although more ova increase the chance of pregnancy, the consequences can be problematic. Not all couples are glad to have triplets or quadruplets, although others are more favourably inclined to the prospect.
7. This description of the course of events is based on the informants' accounts. It agrees with my own experience from fieldwork. I have taken part, for instance, in a number of *in vitro* fertilization operations.
8. This technologization of the body has been criticized by many women's organizations. The technology is described, for example, by the Feminist International Network of Resistance to Reproductive and Genetic Engineering (FINRRAGE) as scientific exploitation of the female body (*Kvinnovetenskaplig tidskrift* 1986/4; see also Corea 1985; Weimarck 1986/4; Nordborg 1991).
9. Fertilization outside the body and the potential to choose the sex of the child is not without controversy in England; the issue has been debated in literature and the media (see Giovanni in *The Sunday Times*, 17/7 1994).
10. The will to define a person's exact genetic origin and hence his or her place in the family structure is revealed, for example, in linguistic usage. Where English has the general term *grandmother* and German *Großmutter*, Swedish has to specify whether it is *mormor* (mother's mother) or *farmor* (father's mother).
11. Ideas about parenthood, that is, the cultural construction of the family, have varied through time and place. Blood ties are not always a precondition for kinship. Anthropological studies have shown how fictive practices can maintain ties of parenthood and kinship in a similar way to genetic bonds (cf. Strathern & Franklin 1993).
12. Insemination Act (1984:1140), External Fertilization Act (1988:71).
13. Sperm donation is permitted in Sweden; if the male in a couple is sterile, sperm can be donated by an outsider. Ovum donation, however, is prohibited by law. The report of the government inquiry into artificial fertilization describes it as "far too unnatural" to allow, for example, a woman with defective fallopian tubes to give birth (Nordborg 1991; SOU 1985:5). There is however a heated debate since some people want to change this law.
14. In Sweden some 250,000 couples, or 500,000 people, are registered as involuntarily childless. The figure comprises people of fertile age. Over

and above this is a large dark figure, which includes people who have chosen not to register their childlessness. The dark figure also includes those who have passed the fertile age and who never became grandparents.

15. This attitude is reminiscent of interviews with women who have undergone beauty operations. Like many childless women, they refuse to accept their destiny. The argument is that identity is inside the body but must be manifested on the surface (Davis 1992; cf. also Lindqvist, "Kvinnligt åldrande, skönhet och könsidentitet", 1996; Ziehe 1989).
16. Associations between Swedish culture and the view of nature and have been discussed in detail by Orvar Löfgren (1987). In this connection it would be worth developing his perspective and asking what associations there are between this view of nature and the specifically Swedish aspiration to create as biologically "natural" family as possible.
17. The discussion thus concerns people's relation to dead *bodies* in late modern society. The actual problematic of dying lies outside this sphere, as does ritual behaviour associated with death and burial. Dying in modern institutional care has been studied in Swedish ethnology by Ferrer-Marine (1981) and is the theme of an ongoing research project entitled "Death as a Cultural Construction" under the leadership of Finnur Magnússon, Lund University. Death and burial in historical perspective is a classic research field in ethnology, which has been studied in detail by Nils-Arvid Bringéus (e.g. 1987, 1994). See also Hagberg 1937.

    Research into death and dying is an expanding field at present. For international references see, e.g., Huntingdon & Metcalf 1979; Cederroth, Corlin & Lindström 1988; Clark 1993; and the journal *Terraine* for 1992, 1993.
18. The view of the taboo on death in modern society is expressed, for example, by Ariès (1974), but his perspective has been criticized on historical grounds, partly for his romantic attitude to dying in the past. For a survey see Hagen 1984.
19. The frequency of autopsies in recent decades has been between 30 and 40 per cent of the total number of deaths in Sweden. From a peak of 48 per cent in 1975, the frequency has decreased. In 1988 the figure was 33 per cent. A constant feature in autopsy statistics is that more men than women undergo post mortems, the difference being about 10 per cent. There are also large regional differences in Sweden. In 1985 the frequency was highest in Malmö municipality, at 77 per cent, while in the counties of Skaraborg and Gotland it was no more than 19 per cent (statistics from SOU 1992:16, p. 114).

    Sweden has long been known for its high autopsy frequency. The figures above can be compared with the 8 per cent for New York. In Sweden anatomical dissections and attendance at autopsies are obligatory elements in medical education. An American study showed that 58 per cent of 136 educational institutions did not demand this (SOU 1992:17, p. 102). This naturally affects the frequency of autopsies, as well as the great variations in practice between different hospitals. Even in Sweden the frequency of autopsies varies not just between regions but also between different departments of the same hospital (SOU 1992:16, p. 114). Besides the role of doctors, there are interesting differences between Sweden and the USA as regards the attitude of relatives to autopsy. A comparison between a Swedish (1973) and an American (1989) study showed that 80 per cent of Swedish relatives granted consent for autopsy, compared with 44 per cent in the USA (SOU 1992:17, pp. 67ff.). The positive Swedish attitude to autopsy still persisted in Margareta Sanner's study in 1992. Sanner's concluding discussion shows that there is not the same positive view of organ donation: "few people question the value of autopsy. This work is not regarded as controversial in the same way as, say, transplantation. The long tradition and the sometimes compulsory nature of autopsies has had the effect of creating a norm which makes them accepted in a way that transplants are not" (Sanner, SOU 1992:17, p. 137).

    From 1 July 1996 a new transplantation law has been in force, in which the principle of "presumed consent" applies. Before the law was introduced, the National Board of Health and Welfare sent forms to everyone in Sweden, asking them to state their attitude to organ donation. An unexpectedly large number of responses were received, many of them positive. Some people, however, made the reservation that their organs should not be given to, for example, foreigners, people outside the family, and the like, even though the law does not admit any such exceptions. The new law has been discussed and criticized from many quarters. One serious objection is that silence in the shape of a failure to respond is interpreted as a positive attitude. The board has nevertheless ensured that the right of relatives to veto organ donation will still obtain in future.
20. Records in the Lund University Folklife Archive, M3145:1, M3989:184, M3620:9.
21. There are exceptions here: the Greek and Syrian Orthodox churches and the Assyrian church (SOU 1992:16, p. 358).
22. The art historian Torsten Weimarck has devoted several works to the analysis of the way anatomy – and ultimately medicine – became a modern model science. It represents a world-view governed by reason, which denies an animistic or magical view of the wholeness of the worldly body. Public anatomical dissections, which were conducted for the first time in Sweden in 1677,

presupposed that the body on the autopsy table "was not a person but a soulless corpse" (1988:299) and hence made a sharp distinction between body and soul. In the dead body one could "read, no longer about destiny and cosmic prospects, but about something very secular and seemingly concrete, namely, the state of health" (1988:295). According to Weimarck, the idea of health replaced the hope of salvation. These ideas are developed further in Weimarck's recently published major work, *Akademi och anatomi* (1996).

23. Cf. Finnur Magnússon's article "Att hitta rätt i ett tomrum" (Finding Your Way in a Vacuum), to be published in 1996.

References

Åkesson, Lynn 1991: *De ovanligas betydelse.* Stockholm: Carlssons.

Arditti, Rita, Renate Duelli Klein & Shelley Minden 1984: *Test-Tube Woman: What Future for Motherhood?* London: Pandora Press.

Ariès, Philippe 1978: *Döden. Föreställningar och seder i västerlandet från medeltiden till våra dagar.* Stockholm: Tidens förlag.

Assier-Andrieu, Louis 1994: L'homme sans limites: Bioétique et anthropologie. *Ethnologie française* 1994/1.

Bloch, Maurice & Jonathan Parry (eds.) 1989: *Death and the Regeneration of Life.* Cambridge: Cambridge University Press.

Bringéus, Nils-Arvid 1987: *Livets högtider.* Stockholm: LT.

Bringéus, Nils-Arvid 1994: Vår hållning till döden. In: *Dödens riter*, ed. by Kristina Söderpalm. Stockholm: Carlssons.

Brinsden, Peter & Paul Rainsbury 1992: *A Textbook of In Vitro Fertilization and Assisted Reproduction.* Cranforth: The Parthenon Publishing Group.

Cederroth, S., C. Corlin & J. Lindström (eds.) 1988: *On the Meaning of Death: Essays on Mortuary Rituals and Eschatological Beliefs.* Uppsala: Almqvist & Wiksell International.

Clark, David (ed.) 1993: *The Sociology of Death: Theory, Culture, Practice.* Oxford: Blackwell Publishers.

Corea, Gena 1985: *The Mother Machine: Reproductive Technologies from Artificial Insemination to Artificial Wombs.* New York: Harper & Row.

Davies, Kathy 1993: Public Appearance, Private Suffering, Cosmetic Surgery and the Female Body. Paper for the conference "Body Images, Language & Physical Boundaries". Amsterdam 1993.

Douglas, Mary 1979: *Purity and Danger: An Analysis of the Concept of Pollution and Taboo.* London: Routledge & Kegan Paul.

Edwards, Janette 1993: Explicit Connections: Ethnographic Enquiry in North-West England. In: *Technologies of Procreation: Kinship in the Age of Assisted Conception,* ed. by Mailyn Strathern. Manchester: Manchester University Press.

Featherstone, Mike 1992: The Body in Consumer Culture. In: *The Body: Social Process and Cultural Theory,* ed. by Mike Featherstone, Mike Hepworth & Brian S. Turner. London: Sage Publications.

Ferrer-Mariné, Julio 1981: *I väntan på döden: En etnologisk undersökning av åldringarnas situation på en långvårdsavdelning.* Stockholm: Akademilitteratur.

Foucault, Michel 1991: *The Birth of the Clinic: An Archaeology of Medical Perception.* London: Routledge.

Frykman, Jonas 1981: Pure and Rational. The Hygienic Vision: A Study of Cultural Transformation in the 1930's. *Ethnologia Scandinavica.*

Frykman, Jonas 1994a: Kroppens förvandlingar: Hälsa, medicin och kulturell förändring i 1900-talets samhälle. *Kulturella perspektiv* 2.

Frykman, Jonas 1994b: On the Move. The Struggle for the Body in Sweden in the 1930s. In: *The Senses Still,* ed. by Nadia Seremetakis. Boulder: West View Press.

Giddens, Anthony 1993: *Modernity and Self-Identity: Self and Society in the Late Modern Age.* Cambridge: Polity Press.

Giovanni, Janine 1994: Bitter Legacy of the Sexual Revolution. *The Sunday Times* 17/7 1994.

Gonzalez-Crussi, F. 1993: *The Day of the Dead and Other Mortal Reflexions.* Orlando: Harcourt Brace & Company.

Hagberg, Louise. 1937: *När döden gästar: Svenska folkseder och svensk folktro i samband med död och begravning.* Stockholm: Wahlström & Widstrand.

Hagen, Rune 1984: Historien om mentaliteterna. En introduktion av Annales-skolans mentalitetshistoriska forskning och en presentation av skolans främsta mentalitetshistoriker. *Häften för kritiska studier* 1/84.

Haraway, Donna 1992: *Primate Visions: Gender, Race and Nature in the World of Modern Science.* London/New York: Verso.

Huntington, R. & P. Metcalf 1979: *Celebrations of Death: The Anthropology of Mortuary Rituals.* Cambridge University Press.

Kemp, Peter 1991: *Det oersättliga: En teknologietik.* Stehag/Stockholm: Symposion.

Kildegaard, Bjarne 1985: Unlimited Memory: Photography and the Differentiation of Familiar Intimacy. *Ethnologia Scandinavica.*

af Klintberg, Bengt 1994: *Den stulna njuren: Sägner och rykten i vår tid.* Stockholm: Norstedts.

Lag 1984:1140: *Om insemination.*

Lag 1988:71: *Om befruktning utanför kroppen.*

Lasch, Christopher 1977: *Haven in a Heartless World: The Family Besieged.* New York: Basic Books.

Lindqvist, Beatriz 1996: Kvinnligt åldrande, skönhet och könsidentitet. In: *Kroppens tid*, ed. by Susanne Lundin & Lynn Åkesson. Stockholm: Natur & Kultur.

Löfgren, Orvar 1987: The Nature Lovers. In: *Culture Builders: A Historical anthropology of Middle-Class Life,* by Jonas Frykman & Orvar Löfgren. New Brunswick, N.J.: Rutgers University Press.
Lundin, Susanne 1987: Hälsokultur. In: *Mera än mat,* ed. by Anders Salomonsson. Stockholm: Carlssons.
Lundin, Susanne & Lynn Åkesson 1994: Kroppens förvandlingar. *LundaLinjer* 111.
Lundin, Susanne & Lynn Åkesson (ed.) 1996: *Kroppens tid.* Stockholm: Natur & Kultur. (To appear in English as The Time of the Body. Lund University Press.)
Magnússon, Finnur.1996: Den äckelsköna döden. *Kulturella perspektiv* 1996:2.
Melucci, Alberto 1992: *Nomader i nuet: Sociala rörelser och individuella behov i dagens samhälle.* Göteborg: Daidalos.
Mestrovic, Stjepan, G. 1993: *The Barbarian Temperament: Toward a Postmodern Critical Theory.* London/New York: Routledge.
Moravec, Mark 1993: Organ Kidnap Legends. *Australian Folklore* 8.
Nordborg, Gudrun 1991: Läkarmakten över moderskapet. *Retfærd* 52.
Rapp, Raina 1993: Accounting for Amniocentesis. In: *Knowledge, Power & Practice: The Anthropology of Medicine and Everyday Life,* ed. by Lindenaum & Lock. University of California Press.
Rosenbeck, Bente 1989: Den mytiska biologin. *Häften för kritiska studier* 1/89.
Sachs, Lisbeth 1993: Sjukdom, diagnos och terapi: En kamp mellan onda och goda krafter. In: *Ondskans etnografi,* ed. by Lena Gerholm & Tomas Gerholm. Stockholm: Carlssons.
Salomonsson, Anders 1987: Det vegetariska alternativet. In: *Mera än mat,* ed. by Anders Salomonsson. Stockholm: Carlssons.
Saynor, James 1993: TV's Pathological Obsession with Death. *The Observer* 19/12 1993.
Serrano, Andres 1993: *The Morgue.* Paris: Galerie Yvon Lambert.
SOU. Statens offentliga utredningar 1985:5: *Barn genom befruktning utanför kroppen.*
SOU. Statens offentliga utredningar 1989:51: *Den gravida kvinnan och fostret – två individer: Om fosterdiagnostik: Om sena aborter.*
SOU. Statens offentliga utredningar 1989:99: *Organdonation och transplantation – psykologiska aspekter.*
SOU. Statens offentliga utredningar 1992:16: *Kroppen efter döden.*
SOU. Statens offentliga utredningar 1992:17: *Den sista undersökningen – obduktionen i ett psykologiskt perspektiv.*
Strathern, Marilyn 1993a: A Question of Context. In: *Technologies of Procreation: Kinship in the Age of Assisted Conception,* ed. by Mailyn Strathern. Manchester: Manchester University Press.
Strathern, Marilyn 1993b: A Relational View. In: *Technologies of Procreation: Kinship in the Age of Assisted Conception,* ed. by Mailyn Strathern. Manchester: Manchester University Press.
Strathern, Marilyn & Sara Franklin 1993: *Kinship and the New Genetic Technologies: An Assessment of Existing Anthropological Research.* University of Manchester: Dept of Social Anthropology.
Terraine. Carnets du patrimoine ethnologique. No. 18, 1992: *Le Corpes en morceaux.*
Terraine. Carnets du patrimoine ethnologique. No. 20, 1993: *La Mort.*
Tracy, Robert 1990: Loving You All Ways: Vamps, Vampires, Necrophiles and Necrofilles in Nineteenth-Century Fiction. In: *Sex and Death in Victorian Literature,* ed. by Regina Barreca. London: Macmillan Press.
Turner, Victor 1985: *The Ritual Process: Structure and Anti-Structure.* New York: Cornell University Press.
Weimarck, Ann-Charlotte 1986: Fortplantningsteknologier – etik och kvinnosyn. *Kvinnovetenskaplig tidskrift* 1986/4.
Weimarck, Torsten 1988: Table et tableau. *Res Publica.*
Weimarck, Torsten 1996: *Akademi och Anatomi.* Stehag/Stockholm: Symposion.
Wirtberg, Ingegärd 1992: *His and Her Childlessness.* Stockholm: Karolinska institutet.
Ziehe, Thomas 1989: *Kulturanalyser: Ungdom, utbildning, modernitet.* Stehag/Stockholm: Symposion.

The Consumption of 'Touching' Images

Reflections on Mimetic 'Wildness' in the West

Jojada Verrips

Verrips, Jojada 1996: The Consumption of 'Touching' Images. Reflections on Mimetic 'Wildness' in the West. – Ethnologia Europaea 1996: 51–64.

This article examines several mimetic manifestations of excessive 'wildness' in Western societies and cultures. It focuses on their appearance in novels, (horror)films, theatrical plays, ballets, operas, pop music, videogames, digital highways and the metaphysical funfair attraction Virtual Reality. The hypothesis is launched that one cannot properly understand the outburst of 'wildness' in these different genres without paying attention to the tabooization of touching others whom one wants to love or redress. Through the consumption of 'wild' products one remains in *con-tact* with an essential dimension of the self. Finally it is argued one should systematically study the relation between 'wild' and 'civilized' phenomena in order to avoid an overemphasis on our degree of civilization.

Professor Jojada Verrips, Anthropological-Sociological Center, University of Amsterdam, Oudezijds Achterburgwal 185, NL–1012 DK Amsterdam, The Netherlands.

"Wer heute auf sich aufmerksam machen will, tut gut daran, Grenzen zu überschreiten. Am besten die des 'guten Geschmacks.' Doch was schockiert uns denn noch, nach Benetton-Werbe-Kampagnen, bei denen ein sterbender Aids-kranker oder ein Mafia-Opfer in der Blutlache den Absatz von Freizeitmode in die Höhe treibt?" (Stern 42, 14.10.93)

"And this is the métier of the anthropologist. He has to break down the barriers of race and cultural diversity; he has to find the human being in the savage; he has to discover the primitive in the highly sophisticated Westerner of today, and, to see that the animal, and the divine as well, are to be found everywhere in man" (Malinowski 1966:vii).

Introduction[1]

Already for some time I have been trying to develop what I have called 'the anthropology of the wild [in the] West' (cf. Verrips 1993a). Actually this means that I attempt to chart, and gain insight in, the 'dark' sides of Western civilization. One of my starting points is that ethnologists, anthropologists, and sociologists up till now have paid too little attention to the 'uncivilized' or 'wild' facets of Western societies and cultures in past and present. However, the number of social scientists involved in mapping out and analyzing these intriguing facets is growing (cf., for example, Duerr 1988, 1990, 1993; Zulaika 1988, 1993; Zijderveld 1991; Feldman 1991; Mestrović 1993; Port 1994; Bax 1995).[2] It won't do to close our eyes for the 'wild' reverse of the proces of civilization in past and present as well as for the presence of 'wild' men and women *among* and, more importantly, *in* our forbears and each of us. For the civilization process does not push aside 'wildness,' but rather runs parallel to the history of that 'wildness,' to its manifestations in an actual and mimetic, that is, fictive re-presented sense (cf. Bartra 1991:120; 1994:145).[3]

As yet I see two reasons why it may be very relevant to focus on the 'uncivilized' facets of Western societies and cultures. Firstly, not only European history, but also our present time abounds with gruesome manifestations of 'wild' or 'uncivilized' behavior. Secondly, in the West there currently appears a proliferation of collective re-presentations of and fantasies about 'uncivilized' people who with pleasure break all sorts of sexual taboos and act very violently in different fields, in other words people who do not at all respect the physical integrity of other persons' bodies. Such fantasies are not only encountered in and consumed through such classical genres as (biblical) myths, fairy tales, folk narratives, novels or the art of painting and sculpture, but also through theatrical and opera performances, pop-music, movies in cinemas and on TV, and, recently, also through videogames in gambling-dens or sitting-rooms, CD-Is and CD-ROMs and, last but not least, all sorts of digital highways and virtual reality machines. As a result of technological progress the number of media through which one can receive notice of, be confronted with, and even be actively involved in this kind of mimetic manifestations of 'wildness' increases rapidly. It seems that technology offers a variety of new ways to make use of leisure time.[4]

It is striking that to a large extent this pastime is dominated by the supply and consumption of particular collective re-presentations and fantasies. As I already remarked they pertain to two areas: excessive sex and excessive violence or a combination of the two, in other words, *eros* and *thanatos*, matters as old as humanity. This brings me to a short clarification of my terminology, in particular my use of the terms 'wild' and 'wildness' as opposed to 'civilized.'[5] For me 'wildness' in a formal etic sense refers to taboo-breaking or excessive (collective) re-presentations and fantasies, especially with regard to sex and/or violence, and their enactment in mimetic as well as actual ways. This means that the particular emic content of 'wildness' in a mimetic and actual sense is context dependent and has to be studied from case to case. Thus, I use the term in a sensitizing sense, in the same way as its counterpart 'civilized.' 'Wildness' so conceived can be a very patterned and far from chaotic, unstructured phenomenon. In other words, there can be a lot of method or system in the 'wildness.' The main question this paper will address is why people nowadays seem to be inclined to increasingly produce and consume all sorts of 'wild' products of a mimetic nature. But first I shall illustrate how 'wildness' currently crops up in novels, strips, theatre and opera performances, (video)movies and videoclips, the hardrock and heavy metal scene, videogames and the farthest corners of the digital and virtual landscape, in short, in the recreational (techno)sphere. Next I shall try to explain the enormous popularity of the excessive representation of sex and violence as recreative means of people who usually regard themselves as considerably or even hyper-'civilized' and who would probably become rather angry if one would dare to compare them – to take a far away cross-street – with the members of a so-called 'primitive' or 'savage' tribe in New Guinea. In my interpretation I will mainly concentrate on the sort of experience that is at issue in the consumption of these representations. I will not deal in this article with all sorts of actual 'wildness,' that is excessive violent behavior resulting in really hurting the physical integrity of others.

'Wild' products and their consumption

Let me start my short tour with a recent literary product in which the reverse of everything that borders upon civilization has been put into words in utmost detail: Bret Easton Ellis' best-seller *American Psycho*. In that novel we encounter in a bewildering yet fascinating fashion a modern version of Dr Jekyll and Mr Hyde in the shape of the New York yuppie Patrick Bateman, who has taken to tear into pieces, barbecue or cut up people, above all beautiful young women (so-called 'hard bodies'), or to kill them in other brutal ways. *American Psycho* is a full-fledged, modern variant of the work of De Sade, a work which, by the way, still is extremely popular and which forms the source of inspiration for the manufacture of all sorts of products of the imagination from strips to movies (cf. *Der Spiegel* 4.06.90). In a magnificent essay about *American Psycho* the anthropologist Marina de Vries says the following:

"Ellis describes the events with so much detail that your heart starts beating faster and the need to vomit is closer than laughter. You quickly read further to take up the thread of daily dawdling with relief and feel almost blessed.

American Psycho is not just a book. It is terribly shocking, hallucinating and exciting. (...) Ellis makes us face the facts and shows us who we are: civilized monsters" (1993:114 – translation JV).

The monstrous in Ellis' novel is shocking, but attractive and exciting at the same time.[6]

The same can be said with regard to strips-for-adults-only, which often excel through bizarre sex, not rarely in combination with a considerable sort of gruesome, graphic violence. But also in cartoons for children one may encounter forms of terrible violence applied to the human body which are hardly inferior to the violence exposed in adults' strips. A good example forms the stickeralbum *The Sloppy Slobs* for which my neighbor's young sons recently bought plates with much enthusiasm from the authorized tobacconist in the neighborhood. These plates offer a large series of illustrations of ill-treated, disintegrated, scalped, exploded, fried, cut up and pierced children's bodies.

A true treasure-house of extreme violations of existing taboos with regard to sex and violence are movies, above all the genre of the horror film that became the vogue in the 1930s (cf. Twitchell 1985; Tudor 1989). In the last fifteen years this genre has reached a hitherto unknown popularity and there seems to come no end to the inventivity of the makers as to let blood flow and bodies transform or disintegrate in a monstrous way, often after being sexually abused intensively. One common feature of many horror films is the almost unbridled violence towards the human body which they show extensively (cf. Verrips 1993b). Here emerge the ultimate antipodes of the 'civilized' Westerner[7] who knows to master his impulses and treats his neighbors decently. Currently, for example, there is much talk about what has been called the phenomenon of the 'nouvelle violence' in films. Who is not familiar with the discussions about Oliver Stones' movie *Natural Born Killers* in which a young couple sends more than fifty persons into death and about the taboo-breaking films of the Ex-South African Ian Kerkhof which depicts utmost extreme forms of violence and sexuality? Other examples of extremely violent recent movies are, among others, *C'est Arrivé Près de Chez Vous, Reservoir Dogs, Pulp Fiction, Henry, Portrait of a Serial Killer, La Haine* and *The Doom Generation.*[8] About the maker of *Pulp Fiction* Quentin Tarantino the journalist Kristine Kruttschnitt remarked:

"Seine Fusion von Subkulturgut und Gangsterfilm *trifft wie die Faust das Auge* einer Zuschauer-Generation, die gelangweilt ist von den immergleichen, immersüssen Märchen aus der Traumfabrik" (*Stern* 44, 1994 – emphasis JV).

Recently theatrical performances have also come up with seminal, taboo-breaking depictions of sex and violence, in short, the exposition of awe-inspiring naked and/or destructed bodies. In this context the so-called 'faeces dramas' of the Austrian dramatist Werner Schwab[9] have to be mentioned immediately, namely *Overweight unimportant: without form, The presidents, Holocaust, or my liver is senseless* and *My dogmouth* (translation JV). In the last years, these shocking plays were performed in the Netherlands by theatrical company *De Trust*. In the first play *Overweight unimportant* a couple is raped, murdered atrociously and devoured by a number of horrible pub-crawlers. In the *Cultural Supplement (CS)* of the Dutch newspaper *NRC Handelsblad* (26.08.94) Joyce Roodnat wrote the following about the public watching the play:

"Some people continued listening while averting their eyes, others left the hall ghastly...many a person, however, could not help but be *watching and listening* – tremulously but with fascination – to where horror and lunacy led" (translation and emphasis JV).

About the tenor of the play *The Presidents* Pieter Kottman stated in November 1993: "It is comparable with that of '*Without Form*': Man is a wolf towards man and apparent civilization always loses on the inclination towards violence" (translation JV). But next to Schwab there are similar playwrights[10], for example, the Flemish dramatist Franz Marijnen, who transformed two narratives of Bataille *(Histoire de l'Oeil* and *Le Mort)* into one play (titled

Bataille/bataille) for the *Noord Nederlands Toneel* (NNT) in 1992. Central to that play is the dark side of eroticism or how voluptuousness can lead to violence and murder. In an interview Marijnen remarked that he had read Bataille's stories "with increasing unbelief, with a feeling as if my intestines were torn out. All of a sudden everything bourgeois morals prescribed were thoroughly turned upside down" *(NRC Handelsblad* 9.10.92, translation JV). And this he wanted to show in a shocking manner in his stage version of these narratives. Shortly before the performance he remarked:

"Our performance has to slide on without anything being able to stop it, as it were, so that we break through the membrane of interdictions. (...) If I together with my frolic dogs, as I call the actors caressingly, can transmit such a sort of emotion I am a happy person" (Ibid.).

In this context the scandalizing work *The Law of the Remains* by the American stage-manager of Iranian origin Reza Abdoh, in which next to Andy Warhol the repulsive serial killer Jeffrey Dahmer also figures,[11] may not remain unmentioned. During the performance in the Netherlands the public was almost literally called to join a massacre, for

"The offender scoops hands full of blood out of a bucket he brought with him and as a wild animal he tears into pieces the liver he collects from that same bucket" (*NRC Handelsblad* 5.05.93, translation JV).

In Germany, where the play was performed shortly before, things went probably even more 'wild,' witness the following quote from *Stern*:

"Als Kirchenglocken die Vorstellung einläuten, beginnen für die Zuschauer 90 gehirnerschütternde Minuten. Da rammt sich eine Darstellerin einen silbernen Vibrator in die Vagina. Ihrem Mitspieler wird der Lauf eines Revolvers in den Anus getrieben. Auf zwei Bildschirmen ist eine Autopsie in Grossaufnahme zu sehen. Und mit dem Dezibel-Level eines Speed-Metal-Konzerts rotzt eine glatzköpfige Amazone Rap-Vulgarismen: 'Lick me, stick me, prick me, smash me, rape me, beat me, eat me, fuck me.' Besucher werden in Geiselhaft genommen. Mit barschen Kommandos treiben Ordner die Menge zwischen den vier Bühnen hin und her. Und immer wieder stürzen nackte, blutverspritzende Schauspieler ins Publikum" (nr. 23 3.06.93).[12]

The work of American choreographer Lisa Marcus who is working in the Netherlands suggests that ballet, too, is in the grip of the urge to shift boundaries. Her ballets *Overlust* and *S* drip with eroticism and violence, which is no great wonder if one knows that like Franz Marijnen she received her inspiration from Bataille.

"In theater-dance-productions by Lisa Marcus dancers are to commit themselves. They survey...impudently and sometimes stark naked the boundaries of eroticism" (*Volkskrant* 11.02.94, translation JV).

Recently Peter Greenaway, together with the Dutch composer Louis Andriessen, extended the opera repertoire, wherein of old sex and violence play an important role, with *Rosa, a Horse Drama*. In this modern opera there is much "explicit presentation of cruelty and corporeality" in a way that may elsewhere have caused an enormous scandal. Raymond van den Boogaard answered the question whether Greenaway's first opera contained enough violent sex:

"Indeed! Opera connoisseurs even assure that one of the highlights in this respect, a naked Esmaralda screaming in pains who is taken anally by [her husband] Rosa on stage, in good visibility, forms a primeur in the history of opera" (*CS NRC Handelsblad* 28.10.94, translation JV).

It strikes me that after all Greenaway confronts the public of the opera house with no other images than those which are shown day and night in the porno cinemas and theaters in the center of Amsterdam. I see him as a 'noble' pornographer who cleverly makes use of artistic genres and entourages in order to confront people with what fascinates them over and over again: sex and violence.[13]

In the world of popular music, too, one may notice continuous attempts to shift and surpass boundaries, especially in rock music. This happens through song texts, covers of records and CDs, videoclips as well as the performances given by bands and the names with which they adorn themselves. Especially in the heavy metal scene which, by the way, consists of various subgenres, there are cases that are telling in this respect. In this scene song titles as *Killing is my business ... and business is good, Some heads are gonna roll, Bring your daughter to the slaughter, Eat the rich,* and *Shoot to thrill* are quite normal.[14] On covers of records and CDs one may come across extremely bloody images of people destroyed by biting, cutting or sawing. For instance, the group *Cannibal Corpse* came up with a CD depicting slaughtered children on the cover. The splatter-metal-group *Gwar*, which toured Europe some years ago and also came to Amsterdam, confronted the public with an atrocious horror show, in which it was completely spattered with (imitation) bodily fluids such as blood and sperm.[15]

"Seminal emissions last for minutes and the (menstruation-)blood squirts into the hall for meters (...) The dancer Slymenstra Hymen stabs somebody's eyes with her pointed Bra and the other musicians are enthusiastically tearing off arms, heads and legs.(...) Unsavouriness reaches a climax when a female doll appears on a turning wheel who is assaulted by the singer Balsac the Jaws of Death with his knotty penis" (*NRC Handelsblad* 27.08.92, translation JV).

Someone who did his utmost best to really overcome all taboos pertaining to sex and violence was the punkrocker GG Allin who died in 1993 from an overdose. At one time this man, to whom it became a habit to masturbate and go to stool on stage and throw his faeces into the public, wrote: "I want to go as far as I can to break laws and make blood flow" (*Het Parool* 11.12.93).[16] Fortunately his plan to commit suicide on stage and take part of his public with him into death – a reason why some of his fans accompanied him to any place – was not realized.

These cases are admittedly extreme, but it is my conviction that they reveal much about the other side of the civilization coin. A fascinating phenomenon in this context, which amuses a great number of adolescents (not to speak of adults), is that of the MTV-video-jockeys Beavis and Butt-Head, two teeners with pimples, who continuously give evidence of a complete disrespect with regard to existing norms pertaining to sex and taboos concerning the use of violence. Talking about amusement: what should one think about the immense stream of videogames whose only goal it seems to be to shoot to pulp as many supposed enemies – in human or nonhuman shape – as possible and ... to help its consumers recreate themselves. If one does not wish to make use of it in gambling-dens, whose number has been rising rapidly in the big cities over the last years, after some investments one can do it at home with a gameboy or with a disk or CD-Rom on the PC-screen. The Japanese companies Nintendo and Sega undercut each other in bringing this sort of games on the market. This competition seems to involve large sums, for there is evidently a great demand for games through which one can manifest oneself as a dexterous destroyer of living and lifeless matter. There is a great number of magazines on the market which inform the consumer of videogames about the latest violent game of skill, for example the magazine *Sega Power*. On the cover of the December-issue of 1994 one can read: "Bloody ... violence WARNING DO NOT turn to page 16." Of course the first page I turned up was page 16, and what could one read there? Among other things the following:

"*Doom* is a stalking, raggedly intense meditation on blind, ugly violence. I have under my control an impossibly pumped-up ... fearless BLOKE who has taken it upon his ... muscular self to descend into a nightmarish pit ... to shoot some rather unspeakably evil creatures repeatedly in the forehead."

It would only require little effort to present here an endless list of examples of violent games with appropriate texts similar to the one presented above, but I contend that this quote is sufficient.[17]

In case one is not satisfied with the possibility to chase opponents to the other world on screen, since a short time one can also enter laser labyrinths, in which one can dress in a particular suit and indulge in chasing and killing others with laser pistols.[18] This can be considered as a modern version of the old game of playing with soldiers, a game with which above all little boys amused themselves before this type of technological break-through. However, a striking difference between gameboys and computergames on the one hand and tin soldiers and tanks, and plastic stenguns on the other is that the former do not allow its user to employ much fantasy in being destructive because they are completely programmed in this respect. In the same way as one can witness the destruction of bodies on TV both in reality and fancy, these new games demonstrate this in detail, and with smell and color. The main difference between watching such things on TV and being actively involved in such games is that in the latter case one is the cause of the destruction whilst one consumes it passively in the former.

Finally I would like to briefly go into manifestations of 'wildness' in the enormously expanding cyberspace and the world of virtual reality. In recent times, quite a few travellers in the cyberspace have not only used the diverse digital 'highways' for decent and 'civilized' purposes, but also – and as it seems increasingly – for the exploration of one's less 'civilized' sides. And we find that, even in this completely new space, which – as the Dutch comedians Koot & Bie have shown so magnificently – one can enter from the bed, the old familiar phenomena reappear: perverse sex and bizarre violence. Internet, currently one of the most important digital highways harbours dark rooms in which 'wildness' reigns supreme. Coen van Zwol wrote about this phenomenon:

"Filthy talk is all the vogue. Recently the paper *Wired* presented an overview on the ten most popular news-groups on the Internet. Among the top seven four were about sex, with half a million to 370,000 readers. There are all sorts of sex groups: bondage, watersport fetishism and bestialities... Often under pseudonym such matters are discussed as the use of sanding machines in masturbation, or anal sex with German sheep-dogs" (*NRC Handelsblad* 13.08.94, translation JV).

According to the journalist Francisco van Jole who regularly reports about what happens on that digital highway Internet is "worse than marquis De Sade" (translation JV). He called the newsgroup *alt.tasteless* a "musty dump area" in which

"... is discussed what nobody dares to say in society. Shit and piss form a permanent part of the daily menu, but also fantasies about sex with corpses, ill-treatment of epileptics, all sorts of sacrilege, and the consumption of vomit, to give just a few prudent examples" (*Volkskrant* 20.06.94, translation JV).

Thus, also in the cyberspace the maltreated naked and destroyed body appears in all vehemence and there, too, people amuse themselves by writing about it and/or looking at it.[19] In the Netherlands a certain Mo Vollebregt manages the company *Intensive Care Computer-informatie BV* through which it is possible to enjoy sex by computer in a way similar to PTT sex-lines (*VPRO-gids* 39 24/30.09.94).[20] A quickly expanding phenomenon, at least if we may believe Van Jole, is 'digital turtling' or entering into a 'net relationship' with a 'fellow-traveller' in the cyberspace. For example, via Internet Relay Chat people know to arouse each other to large heights; electro-romanticism flourishes, because people exchange intimate things which one would not utter easily elsewhere (*Volkskrant* 9.07.94).[21] According to Van Jole next to anonymity this is due to the absence of "any stimulation of the senses." I shall shortly make clear that I do not agree with this.

A field in which technicians are busy to approximate reality as closely as possible and to offer users utmostly complete experiences is that of virtual reality. Also in this field violence and sex appear in a way similar to the genres mentioned earlier on. At the moment there are two types of VR: one which one can experience via a stereohelmet, a glove and even a complete dress (cybersuit), and one which one can experience in a videodrome. Especially in the case of the first variant all sorts of laboratory experiments take place with regard to sexual stimulation. For example, there are attempts to accompany the process of *looking* at three-dimensional images of beautiful (naked) men and women with the adequate *feeling* of sexual arousal by way of a costume full of refined *sensors*.

"By way of a helmet with glasses and headphones the user is led into the virtual world visually; on the screen a partner appears, whose image is based on a photo model, a film star or a true sweetheart. Gloves (*datagloves*) and a penis quiver or teledildo are to do the rest. Stimuli are passed on electrically under the *datasuit* to the body part concerned and diverge from maximally 3,5 volt for a slight touch to maximally 49 volt for the lovers of a more hard approach" (Spaink *De Groene* 20.07.94, translation JV).

What we face here is an extremely intricate technical manifestation of a mechanics of masturbation, an ingenious combination of bodily lust experience and technological genius. Let me, by the way, remark, that one reaches here the fascinating field of the sexual relation(ship) between human beings and things (above all machines), or, put differently, the mechanization of sex and the erotization of the machine.[22]

Whereas in the case mentioned above a single person entertains himself or herself, there are currently also experiments with persons in cyber- or datasuits, who try to arouse each other at a distance by way of electronic impulses which are evoked by computers and passed on via modems and telephones (Spaink *De Groene* 20.07.94). In 1990 Howard Rheingold wrote an article titled *Teledildonics: Reach out and touch someone*:

"Twenty years from now, when portable teledidlers are ubiquitous, people will use them to have sexual experiences with *other people*, at a distance, in combinations and configurations undreamt of by precybernetic voluptuaries. Through the synthesis of virtual reality technology and telecommunication networks, you will be able to reach out and touch someone ... in ways humans have never before experienced" (1990:52).

He advocated to call the technology necessary to develop this experience "tactile telepresence." However, the development of this sort of technology is still in its infancy.[23] With this I have finished my brief overview of mimetic manifestations of 'wildness' in a number of recreative genres or media, ranging from novels to VR.[24]

Discussion

It is striking, that again and again these manifestations seem to concern the same two matters: (excessive) sexuality and violence, the manhandled naked and awfully destructed body, or *eros* and *thanatos*. All the time it is the 'wild' 'caress' of and 'blow' on the body, so to speak, which fascinates people so much that they entertain themselves by *looking at*, and *listening to*, these manifestations. This fascination is shared by young and old, men and women, and people of all classes, though not always to the same degree and intensity. At most, they differ from each other with respect to the medium through which they prefer to consume the 'wild' 'caress' and 'blow': film or opera, novel or gameboy, laserlabyrinth or VR-helmet. In a review of Paglia's book *Sexual Personae. Art and Decadence from Nefertiti to Emily Dickinson* the critics Gracie & Zarkov postulate the following:

"We sometimes imagine ourselves to be extraterrestrial anthropologists examining the shards of Western Art. What to make of the recurring motif of sex and violence exfoliating through its artifacts?"

And their answer is:

"Jung called it the Shadow – the repressed biological energy of sexual and aggressive drives... The Shadow looms over history, manifesting itself in war, political oppression, and sexual violence. But in the realm of the artist, the Shadow can defuse and amuse, enlighten and instruct" (Gracie & Zarkov 1991:118).

And they are in favor of the latter, because in this way people would be prevented from committing actual misdeeds; fantasizing over sexual outrages, for example, would prevent that they take place in reality. Gracie & Zarkov's idea is very close to Lévi-Strauss' on myths, for according to him in myths extreme positions are represented in order to explain that in practice they are untenable (Lévi-Strauss 1967:30).[25]

A somewhat different view on the fascination with (perverse) sex and (heart-rending) violence, or the 'uncivilized' 'caress' of and 'blow' on the body, is offered by Bataille who inspired quite a few artists as we saw above. For Bataille asserted: "The prohibition exists in order to be violated" (1993:81, translation JV). On the one hand there are all sorts of taboos to warrant the physical integrity of human beings, on the other hand the very existence of these taboos entices the lust to transgress them and to violate the physical integrity of others in order to escape from the negative emotions associated with these taboos and to enjoy the positive emotions associated with trespassing them. Viewed in this way it is possible to interpret the excessive mimetic re-presentations of sex and violence which I sketched earlier as surrogates which are to lead people back to a sort of emotion from which they have become alienated.[26]

However fascinating I find this view, still there is something missing; there is need to extend and aggravate it. Before I start to outline this, I would first like to briefly deal with the question as to what the specific ways in which the mistreated naked and destroyed body currently figures in various genres and media can teach us about the nature of Western societies. For according to Mary Douglas the characteristics of the social body which people form together influence the way in which they perceive the physical body.

"The physical experience of the body, always modified by the social categories through which it is known, sustains a particular view of society. There is a continual exchange of meanings between the two kinds of bodily experience so that each reinforces the categories of the other" (1982:65).

If this is correct, then the frequent appearance of the ill-treated naked and destructed body in all sorts of recreative genres reflects a particular view of society: namely as an extremely fragile and vulnerable whole which can easily be raped, dislocated and destroyed by a number of very 'uncivilized' 'caresses' and 'blows.' Of course, such a view is embedded in a particular context which only arises under certain societal circumstances, circumstances under which people fear for the maintenance of their own physical integrity. Reasoned in this way, it would be possible to relate the mimetical manifestations of excessive 'wildness' which I dealt with in the last instance to fundamental uncertainties regarding social life in Western societies (cf. Carroll 1990:213). The attraction of these manifestations could then be attributed to the fact that through their consumption people are able to face their own anxieties via the mechanism of projection.[27] Whether this leads to catharsis or rather to an increase of fear is a question with which I do not want to deal here because it would lead us too far off.

Let me now try to indicate what I consider indispensable to gain deeper insight into the fascinating phenomenon that, as I noted above, there is a steady extension of the sort of media with which people entertain themselves in their pastime and yet again and again they fall back on the very ancient themes of sex and violence and an excessive trespassing of the taboos surrounding them. Since I remarked that it would be possible to supplement Bataille's view, I want to end my account by indicating how to do so.

I think that it is important to realize that among the five sensual capacities distinguished in the West, that is, vision, hearing, smell, taste and touch, the so-called 'distance senses' of seeing and hearing prevail over the so-called 'proximity senses' of smelling, tasting and touching (cf. Howes 1991; Synnott 1993:128 ff.; Falk 1994:11). While Westerners were predominantly audio-oral before the invention of bookprinting, afterwards they became increasingly audio-visually oriented. In the West, the experience of the world and everything it contains went more and more by eye and ear. We consider what we hear less reliable than what we see and our ideas about knowledge are closely related to visual perception: we look at something, develop insights, see, have a view or perspective, etcetera (cf. Fabian 1983: ch. 4). Moreover, taking photographs and making videofilms holds a central place in our lives. Among all sensual experiences in our culture the touch is the least valued and feared most.[28] Westerners (and especially people of Christian background) are not in favor of tactility, neither in the positive nor negative sense. As far as that goes our proxemic rules have become very strict. The sexual touch of others except one's own partner (at least if it is not of a rapelike nature) has become a taboo, in the same way as the aggressive touch of others who threaten our feeling of self-esteem, our honor or our physical integrity. Caressing and beating bodies except one's own is generally speaking surrounded by a great number of rules, which one should better respect in order to avoid difficulties with neighbors, the government or both. In the context of showing affection as well as in the context of assuming power, the 'touch' got increasingly ostracized.[29] And this happened despite the fact that the touch can be seen as the most fundamental sensual experience, because it is directly related to the reproduction and protection (possibly by destruction) of the human species (cf. Montagu 1971). The touch also is the most fundamental of all senses, because the four others can be reduced to it, that is, they can be seen as variants of the touch. Seeing, hearing, smelling, and tasting are in the last instance nothing else than tactile processes.

I would like to propose that there is a direct relationship between the imprisonment of the actual 'touch' in Western societies (that is, the tabooization of touching others whom one wants to love or redress) *on the one hand*, and, *on the other*, the recurrence of the two manifestations of mimetic 'wildness' in people's leisure time which I signalled earlier on, namely the 'wild' 'caress' and 'blow' by which the naked body can transform into a terribly destroyed body. In my view it is possible to restrict people's inborn inclination to caress or beat others to some extent, but not in such a way that this inclination ceases to manifest itself at all. The stronger the restrictions, the more ingeniously this inclination seems to crop up through other channels, for example, via the production and consumption of mimetic audiovisual manifestations of sexual and aggressive 'wildness' in order to be *touched by it*.[30] What one is about to lose (in the case of children) or has lost already through learning (in the case of adults) – namely the possibility to touch uninhibitedly in order to love or attack or even to destroy as an act of self-preservation – is retrieved through the intermediation (consumption) of novels, films, theatrical plays, ballets, operas, concerts, videogames, digital highways and the metaphysical funfair attraction Virtual Reality.[31] Thereby one remains in *contact* with an essential dimension of the self which is for social reasons not permissible in its rude, uncultivated form, but which can never be denied or even abolished. In this way, albeit temporarily, we learn to become masters of the world in which we live and are enabled to get rid of the alienation resulting from the imprisonment of our ambivalent tactile needs. I am convinced that the emergence of the naked and destroyed body, of an exuberant *eros* and a horrible *thanatos*, in all sorts of contexts is related to Westerners' desire to not only better *grasp* the world in which they live, but also to get it better into their *grip* than is the case now and ... to be *touched* by it. No civilization without its own sort of recreative (and, alas, actual) 'wildness.' In the West this is above all a mimetic tactile 'wildness' (mediated by the eye and the ear) in the field of sex (the naked body) and aggression (the destructed body), because here the idea prevails that only these persons are really 'civilized' who have learned to keep their hands to themselves, also in their social relations with others in their leisure time.

Notes:

1. Earlier versions of this article were presented at the Congress *Vrijetijd: tussen genot, verbod en verleiding* held in Rotterdam 15–16 December 1994 and at the Fifth Interdisciplinary Conference on Research in Consumption *Learning to Consume* at the Department of European Ethnology Lund University 18–20 August 1995. I want to thank the participants of the latter conference, especially Ayse Caglar, for their critical but constructive comments. I am indebted to Jaap Lengkeek for stimulating remarks, to John Wiersma for directing my attention to a lot of interesting sources and to Birgit Meyer for her indispensable help in clarifying my 'pensée sauvage' with regard to the 'Wild West.'
2. In other disciplines, such as history, English, (comparative) literature, and philosophy the interest in the 'wild' side of Western civilization now and in the recent past also seems to be growing (cf., for example, Twitchell 1985, 1989; Showalter 1991; Massumi 1993; Warner 1994 and Boomkens 1996).
3. A very interesting development is that several epigones of the sociologist Norbert Elias, who became famous for his study (1969) of the civilization process in Europe, recently started with research on processes of 'decivilization.' See, for example, Mennell (1989) and Bax (1995). For a long time they were not interested in the 'wild' reverse of the proces of civilization. For them it formed a kind of residual category, with which they hardly ever dealt as far as the present was concerned and which they pushed to the background and projected back into time in a fashion common among evolutionary anthropologists at the end of the nineteenth century. Typical for these epigones is that they see particular manifestations of 'decivilization' and 'barbarization' as a kind of temporary backsliding and not as structural phenomena running parallel to the civilization process as such or, in other words, never absent uncivilized or 'wild' 'counterpoints' in society and culture.
4. Recently the Dutch philosopher Boomkens (1996) called this whole ensemble of media bombarding us with horrific and shocking images and information the 'angstmachine' ('anxiety-machine'), which he sees, just as some epigones of Elias, as the inevitable outflow of the fact that people live in a very 'civilized' and therefore boring society, which he qualifies as a 'geborgenheidsmachine' ('security machine'). See also the work of Massumi (1993), who emphasizes the political side of this media shower of fearsome imagery.
5. In a nice essay on the occurrence of extreme violence in fairy tales Mallet (1993) uses the same contrast 'wild'/['unzivilisiert'] versus 'zivilisiert.' I fully agree with the last sentence of that essay: 'Wir alle haben eben mehr oder weniger unzivilisierte Regungen, mit denen wir fertig werden müssen, und es ist allemal besser und für den seelischen Haushalt bekömmlicher, um seine Wildheit zu wissen, als sie zu verdrängen oder sich gar einzubilden, nur die anderen seien schlecht.'
6. Of course, the novel of Ellis is just an example; it does not stand by its own. There were and are many writers who produce this kind of 'wild' literary products. In Europe Elfriede Jelinek's works, for example *Lust*, abound with sketches of excessive sex and violence. It would be interesting to examine the relation between gender and writing 'wild' novels. See Armstrong & Tennenhouse (1989) and Howlett & Mengham (1994) for the relation between literature, art and (the history of) violence.
7. In this connection it is interesting to note that Europe is invaded by a particular kind of animation movies from Japan, the so-called *Manga*, in which all sorts of perverted sex and horrific violence are shown, at least if one can lay hands on uncensored copies. In this case the Western consumer is confronted with the ultimate antipodes of the civilized Japanese. It would be interesting to conduct research on the global spread of these and similar products of mimetic 'wildness' and how consumers appropriate them at a local level.
8. All these films are considered ordinary cinema-movies. Next to this, there is a videocircuit in which products with perverse sex and extreme forms of violence abound. It is possible to hire these products of imagination in any videoshop or to order them through specialized shipment-companies. The following quote is an example of an advertisement by such a company (*Psychotronics* nr. 17, 1994): '*SADISTIC SEX, VIOLENCE & TORTURE* * EurAsia Video Search of America, Inc. can help you unlock the floodgate of your filthy desires and make all your depraved dreams come true.'
9. Before turning to writing plays, Schwab was engaged in the creation of works of art made from perishable materials, such as the heads of slaughtered cows. One is reminded here of the shocking happenings of the Austrian artists Mühl, Nitsch and Brus (cf. Durgnat 1972: ch. 13). At present the Briton Damien Hirst is famous in certain avant garde circles for making 'Skulpturen aus zersägten Kühen, fetten Maden und konservierten Fisch-Leibern' (*Stern* 5.05.94) – which is thus not particularly innovative.
10. What I find rather remarkable is that Austria seems to harbour a whole reservoir of Schwab-like playwrights. Elfriede Jelinek wrote plays in which outrageous violence and sex occured, for example *Raststätte oder Sie machens Alle*, which caused a lot of fuss when it was the first time played in Hamburg in January 1995 (cf. *Stern* 26.01.1995). Peter Turrini, sometimes compared

with a 'wild man,' is another one who likes to stage ultra-violent scenes. He did it, for example, in *Alpenglühen* and *Die Schlacht um Wien*. In the last play the main role is played by a murderous band of people who intend to burn down an asylum, but end up killing each other. Gustav Ernst, the creator of a very rough variant of the classical Faust story, and the South German Tankred Dorst, who wrote *Korbes*, a piece full of extreme violence, also fit in this tradition. The work of the filmer Michael Haneke (*Der siebente Kontinent, Benny's Video, 71 Fragmente einer Chronologie des Zufalls*) is of a similar violent nature. It shows the 'wild' side of the Austrian society and culture.

11. The recent widespread interest in serial killers now and in the past, their criminal acts and motives is striking. Except that they play key roles in films, they have also attracted the attention of quite a few popular writers and serious scientists researchers, especially when they practized cannibalism as Dahmer did.
12. A play in which cruelty and sexual perversity also play an eye-catching role is *Before the end [Voor het einde]* by Ramon Gieling, performed in 1993 by Wolfsmond (*NRC Handelsblad* 18.01.93). In this context *The Wedding House Party* by Lodewijk de Boer, in which a ritual murder, incest and discrimination occur, is also interesting (*NRC Handelsblad* 11.11.94). Last but not least I want to mention *Allegro Barbaro* by director Frans Strijards. He commented: 'In *Allegro Barbaro* I have wittingly been looking for a recognizable situation. Look, the human mechanism does not change. When people feel cornered, they exceed boundaries, not even out of conscious cruelty, but because they feel to be put in a hole by powers which they can only fathom half. Their fear makes that escalation takes place. You can simply claim this, but you have to render it *able to be shared' (CS NRC Handelsblad* 26.11.93 – translation JV).
13. In this connection it is interesting to note that frequently it is the kind of bourgeois public visiting taboo-breaking plays and operas abounding with excessive sex and violence that can make a lot of fuss about the corrupting nature of certain films consumed by people not belonging to their social stratum, for example the working class, and advocate the introduction of powerful (legal) measures with respect to their consumption (cf. Verrips 1995).
14. Interesting in this context are the songs by the so-called gangsterrappers, such as Ice-T and Ice-Cube, in which calls for murdering and descriptions of violently killing persons do not form an exception at all. It is bizarre that some of these musicians actually took to the deeds which they describe in their songs (Carvalho *NRC Handelsblad* 28.01.94). See Weinstein (1991:237 ff.) for a refutation of the view that the texts of heavy-metal-songs would stimulate or at least refer to sexual perversion and violence.
15. Often these acts are clearly mimetical manifestations, that is, performances in which rape, abuse of the human body and murder is merely re-presented. Yet a genre of performance exists in which real abuse of the body stands central. This is, for instance, the case in certain SM-shows and fakir-happenings such as the (Jim Rose) *Circus Side Show* in which people demonstrate what sort of violence towards their own body they can endure, from stinging the handle of a spoon into the noose to filling the stomach with a liquid and pumping it out again (*NRC Handelsblad* 16.07.93).
16. It occurs rather frequently that groups splash their public with bodily fluids. For instance, next to abusing the public, the female rock band *L7* who performed in Amsterdam in November 1994 also spit on it (*NRC Handelsblad* 17.11.94).
17. *Doom* recently got a successor in the form of *Quake*, an even more violent game that became an immediate success in the USA. According to Marina Warner in the world of videogames it is no more slyness that is brought into action against brute violence, as happens in all sorts of old myths, but rather the war hero and the fittest survivor (1994:25).
18. This is a variant of the game of shooting at one another with paintpistols, an activity in which some people indulge in particular clubs.
19. In April 1994 a 25-year old employee of the institute of metallurgy at the university of Birmingham was arrested because – without his superiors being aware of it – by way of the university computer he had offered child porno to the users of Internet (*Guardian* 15.04.94).
20. Some more expensive brothels currently make use of computers by way of which it is possible to watch interactive porno-films on CD-ROM (*Volkskrant* 26.09.94).
21. A special phenomenon is the occurrence of the so-called 'cyberrape' or 'digital violation', that is, sexual harassing of persons who enter certain corners of cyberspace under a female name (Karin Spaink *De Groene* 20.07.94). The use of a female name, by the way, does not indicate a person's gender, for on the digital highways 'genderbending' seems to be a normal phenomenon.
22. All over people are reflecting on this problem. Mazlish (1993), for example, is sure that we are heading towards a situation in which the difference between persons and machines is about to wane. After all, human beings are increasingly mechanized (a.o. by way of artificial organs) while machines are increasingly humanized. In 1993 this was the theme of the fifth *Manifestatie voor de instabiele media (NRC Handelsblad* 30.09.93). According to the American cultural critic Mark Dery the erotization of the machine and the mechanization of sex are currently in full

swing (1991:42 ff.). One response to the rise of cyborgs or post-humans is, in his view, modern primitivism, that is, the trend which is focused on 'the remapping of corporeal territory' by way of 'piercing, binding, "tribal tattooing," and ritual scarification' (1992:103). See in this context also the special issue of *Re / Research* (Primitives 1989) which is devoted completely to these modern primitives.

23. Touching one another at a distance will remain problematic in the near future. For instance, Myron Krueger, who developed the videodrome technique, wrote: 'It is a pity that tactile feedback, the sensation of surfaces or resistance, is so difficult to realize without awkward, expensive and bulky installations. To make contact with matter and the sensation of touching is very important. This is the greatest challenge for the interface designers, but presently it is not yet possible to realize it' (Sala & Barnouw 1990:47/8).
24. It would not have been difficult to extend the series with more genres. Thus I contend that there is a clear family resemblance between watching splatter movies or reading such a novel as *American Psycho*, on the one hand, and practizing disaster-tourism, visiting boxing-matches or cage-fights (where men often hit each other unconscious, beautiful girls – dressed as sparsely as possible – announce rounds and the public is dressed in smokings and evening dresses to emphasize the contrast between the 'wild' and the 'civilized') and other life-threatening sports (such as car and motorbike racing), on the other. For in the latter cases one can also notice this queer combination of excessive *eros* and *thanatos*. A phenomenon which I did not deal with but which fits perfectly in the series is the recent upsurge of reality TV showing all sorts of extreme behavior and activities (e.g. operations on sick bodies) in almost the same way as the mondo 'shockumentaries' so popular in the late sixties.
25. Compare this with the following statement of a boy who was about to hire the videofilm *Faces of Death*: 'True *reality tv*... So you can learn what you are not to do' (*NRC Handelsblad* 8.02.94). If this kind of 'shockumentary' functions in this way, if its (hidden) moral message is rather conservative, then people fearing its morally disrupting effects and campaigning for a stronger censorship should better be glad that they are produced and consumed. See for this kind of interpretation that is in line with Lévi-Strauss' view on myths (and films which he regards as modern myths) Krasniewicz (1992:45/46) and Verrips (1995).
26. By surrendering themselves to (mimetically) trespassing taboos, people come into contact with aspects of themselves from which they have become alienated through the very existence of these taboos. In this sense the consumption of excessive mimetic manifestations of sex and violence or *eros* and *thanatos* could be understood as an interesting and important expedition towards repressed aspects of the self which have a correcting effect on the self image. Through a temporary surrender to or 'possession' by the 'wild' one is able to get to know the 'other' (the 'other' who one also is) within oneself (see also Kramer 1987). Here one touches upon the way in which that what is repressed and surrounded by taboos is evaluated. In the work of Elias it appears to be evaluated in a rather negative sense, whereas in the work of Moscovici, for example, it is valued in more positively (cf. Kielstra 1981).
27. This view sharply contrast with that of Boomkens (1996) who states that the 'anxiety machine' functions because life in our (post-)modern society has become so boring that one needs excessive kicks in the sphere of film, literature and music, etc.
28. "Nichts fürchtet der Mensch mehr als die Berührung durch Unbekanntes. Man will *sehen*, was nach einem greift, man will es erkennen oder zumindest einreihen können. Überall weicht der Mensch der Berührung durch Fremdes aus.(...) Nicht einmal die Kleider gewähren einem Sicherheit genug; wie leicht sind sie zu zerreissen, wie leicht ist es, bis zum nackten, glatten wehrlosen Fleisch des Angegriffenen durchzudringen. Alle Abstände, die die Menschen um sich geschaffen haben, sind von dieser Berührungsfurcht diktiert" (Canetti 1980:9).
29. It is striking that, according to my observation, couples kissing each other in public form less and less part of (urban) street life, at least in the Netherlands. Moreover it has to be noticed that the sexual touch within a marriage can become a dangerous affair for a man, if his wife experiences it as a form of rape. For then she can charge him for that officially (e.g. in Germany) with the consequence that he could end up in jail. Of course, I am not talking of the SM-scene, which seems to be rapidly expanding nowadays and in which this kind of excessive touch amongst other things is especially strived for. In the same way the touching of young children by their parents can become risky, for parents nowadays are rather easily accused of committing incest.
30. Interestingly, the Dutch expression 'beroerd worden' (which I use in the original version of this paper) has two meanings: to become miserable and to be touched. This double meaning captures nicely the implications of people's audiovisual consumption of 'wildness.'
31. In his *magnum opus* Elias postulates a direct relationship between a decrease of the possibilities for individuals to concretely live out their 'Angriffslust' through a process of rigorous tabooization and an increase of a passive, well-mannered desire to watch ('Augenlust') more or less stylized violent sports events, such as boxing

and football matches, instead. "Die Kampf- und Angriffslust findet z.B. einen gesellschaftlichen erlaubten Ausdruck im sportlichen Wettkampf. Und sie äussert sich vor allem in 'Zusehen', etwa im Zusehen bei Boxkämpfen, in der tagtraumartigen Identifizierung mit einigen Wenigen, denen ein gemässigter und genau geregelter Spielraum zur Entladung solcher Affekte gegeben wird. Und dieses Ausleben von Affekten im Zusehen oder selbst im blossen Hören ... ist ein besonders charakterischer Zug der zivilisierten Gesellschaft. Er ist mitbestimmend für die Entwicklung von Buch und Theater, entscheidend für die Rolle des Kinos in unserer Welt" (1969 Erster Band: 280). Though my main argument may appear to resemble that of Elias, the main difference is that I refuse to subordinate the 'wild' to the 'civilized' and thus regard the inclination to watch and/or listen to all sorts of excessive mimetic 'wildness' as merely another indicaton of a high degree of civilization. I reject the idea that one can discern a kind of unilinear evolution from 'Angriffslust' to 'Augenlust' and propagate instead the view that the (actual and mimetic) 'wild' and (actual and mimetic) 'civilized' are always existing next to each other and have to be studied as 'twin-phenomena' or as two sides of the same coin. If one fails to do so one is tempted to exaggerate or underestimate the relevance of the one or the other.

References

Armstrong, N. & L. Tennenhouse 1989: *The Violence of Representation. Literature and the History of Violence*. Cambridge.

Bataille, G. 1993: *De Erotiek*. Transl. Jan Versteeg. Amsterdam.

Bartra, R. 1991: Identity and Wilderness. Ethnography and the History of an Imaginary Primitive Group. In: *Ethnologia Europaea*: 103–25.

Bartra, R. 1994: *Wild Men in the Looking Glass. The Mythic Origins of European Otherness*. Transl. by Carl T. Berrisford. Ann Arbor.

Bax, M. 1995: *Medjugorje: Religion, Politics, and Violence in Rural Bosnia*. Amsterdam.

Boomkens, R. 1996: *De angstmachine. Over geweld in films, literatuur en popmuziek*. Amsterdam.

Canetti, E. 1980: *Masse und Macht*. Frankfurt am Main.

Carroll, N. 1990: *The Philosophy of Horror or Paradoxes of the Heart*. New York & London.

Dery, M. 1991: Guerrilla Semiotics: Sex Machine, Machine Sex: Mechano-Eroticism & Robo-Copulation. In: *Mondo* 5: 42–44.

Dery, M. 1992: Body Politic. In: *Mondo* 6: 101–06.

Douglas, M. 1982: *Natural Symbols. Explorations in Cosmology*. New York.

Duerr, H.P. 1988: *Nacktheit und Scham. Der Mythos vom Zivilisationsprozess*. Frankfurt am Main.

Duerr, H.P. 1990: *Intimität. Der Mythos vom Zivilisationsprozess*. Frankfurt am Main.

Duerr, H.P. 1993: *Obszönität und Gewalt. Der Mythos vom Zivilisationsprozess*. Frankfurt am Main.

Durgnat, R. 1972: *Sexual Alienation in the Cinema. The dynamics of sexual freedom*. London.

Elias, N. 1969: *Über den Prozess der Zivilisation*. 2e Auflage, 2Bd. Bern & München.

Fabian, J. 1983: *Time and the Other. How Anthropology Makes Its Object*. New York.

Falk, P. 1994: *The Consuming Body*. London.

Feldman, A. 1991: *Formations of Violence. The Narrative of the Body and Political Terror in Northern Ireland*. Chicago & London.

Gracie & Zarkow 1991: An Acid Take on Camille Paglia. In: *Mondo* 5: 114–19.

Howes, D. (ed.) 1991: *The Varieties of Sensory Experience. A Sourcebook in the Anthropology of the Senses*. Toronto.

Howlett, J. & R. Mengham (eds.) 1994: *The Violent Muse. Violence and the artistic imagination in Europe, 1910–1939*. Manchester.

Kielstra, N. 1981: Civilisatie of verwildering. Elias, Moscovici en de menselijke natuur. In: *Symposion*: 6–20.

Kramer, F. 1987: *Der rote Fes. Über Besessenheit und Kunst in Afrika*. Frankfurt am Main.

Krasniewicz, L. 1992: Cinematic Gifts: The Moral and Social Exchange of Bodies in Horror Films. In: F.E. Mascia-Lees & P. Sharpe (eds.): *Tattoo, Torture, Mutilation, and Adornment. The Denaturalization of the Body in Culture and Text*. Albany: 30–48.

Lévi-Strauss, C. 1967: The Story of Asdiwal. In: E. Leach (ed.): *The Structural Study of Myth and Totemism*. London: 1–49.

Mallet, C-H. 1993: ...und rissen der schönen Jungfrau die Kleider vom Leibe. Unzivilisierte Regungen in Märchen. In: *Etnofoor*: 93–104.

Malinowski, B. 1966: Introduction. In: J.E. Lips: *The Savage Hits Back*. New York.

Massumi, B. (ed.) 1993: *The Politics of Everyday Fear*. Minneapolis & London.

Mazlish, B. 1993: *The Fourth Discontinuity. The Coevolution of Humans and Machines*. New Haven & London.

Mennell, S.J. 1989: Short-Term Interests and Long-Term Processes: The Case of Civilisation and Decivilisation. In: J. Goudsblom, E.L. Jones & S.J. Mennell (eds.): *Human History and Social Process*. Exeter: 93–127.

Mestrović, S. 1993: *The Barbarian Temperament. Toward a Postmodern Critical Theory*. London & New York.

Montagu, A. 1970: *Touching: The Human Significance of the Skin*. New York & London.

Port, M. v.d. 1994: *Het einde van de wereld. Beschaving, redeloosheid en zigeunercafés in Servië*. Amsterdam.

Primitives 1989: Modern Primitives. An Investigation of Contemporary Adornment & Ritual. *Re/Search* 12. San Francisco.

Rheingold, H. 1990: Teledildonics: Reach out and touch someone. In: *Mondo* 2: 52–56.

Sala, L.H.D.J. & J.P. Barlow 1990: *Virtual Reality. De Metafysische Kermisattractie*. Düsseldorf.

Showalter, E. 1991: *Sexual Anarchy. Gender and Culture at the Fin de Siècle*. London.

Synnott, A. 1993: *The Body Social. Symbolism, Self and Society*. London & New York.

Tudor, A. 1989: *Monsters and Mad Scientists. A Cultural History of the Horror Movie*. Oxford UK & Cambridge USA.

Twitchell, J.B. 1985: *Dreadful Pleasures. An Anatomy of Modern Horror*. New York & Oxford.

Twitchell, J.B. 1989: *Preposterous Violence. Fables of Aggression in Modern Culture*. New York & Oxford.

Verrips, J. 1993a: Op weg naar een antropologie van het wilde westen. In: *Etnofoor*: 5–21.

Verrips, J. 1993b: The Destruction of the Human Body in Horror-Movies. Paper presented at the conference 'Body Images,' Amsterdam, 6–9 July 1993.

Verrips, J. 1995: The State and the Empire of Evil. Paper presented at the 94th Annual Meeting of the AAA at Washington, 15–19 November 1995.

Vries, M. de 1993: American Psycho: 'a piece of shit.' Over nut en nuttiging van schandelijke literatuur. In: *Etnofoor*: 113–22.

Warner, M. 1994: *Managing Monsters. Six Myths of Our Time*. London.

Weinstein, D. 1991: *Heavy Metal. A Cultural Sociology*. New York.

Zulaika, J. 1988: *Basque Violence. Metaphor and Sacrament*. Reno.

Zulaika, J. 1993: Further Encounters with the Wild Man. Of Cannibals, Dogs, and Terrorists. In: *Etnofoor*: 21–41.

Zijderveld, A.C. 1991: Über das Dämonische in der Kultur. In: *Von Weizsäcker Doctor Honoris Causa Erasmus Universität Rotterdam*. Utrecht.

From Passion to Possessiveness

Collectors and Collecting in a Symbolic Perspective

Bjarne Rogan

Rogan, Bjarne 1996: From Passion to Possessiveness. Collectors and Collecting in a Symbolic Perspective. – Ethnologia Europaea 26: 65–79.

Collecting is a pastime that has become immensely popular, especially during the last two or three decades. It is estimated that one in three persons in the adult population in western industrialized countries is or has been a collector. As a pastime collecting easily turns into an engrossing passion or even addiction, with immoderation and sometimes transgression of moral and legal rules in its wake. In popular opinion collecting, even in its moderate and normal forms, is surprisingly often referred to in terms of passion and love and compared to eroticism. So is also the case in fiction, where the collector character abounds. The aim of the article is to discuss the systematic character of rhetorical figures in this discourse on collecting. These figures, most often comparisons and metaphors, are investigated as a symbolic way of understanding the ambiguous phenomena of collecting and possessiveness. As the use of concepts like symbol and symbolism are rather unclear in the ethnological tradition, the author argues for a pragmatic use of some structuralist ideas to grasp their systematic character. This article concentrates upon symbolic perspectives on collecting, whereas the author's research project on collecting comprises topics like gender, consumption, socialization, etc., as well as the history of collecting.

Bjarne Rogan, Professor of Ethnology, University of Oslo, Institutt for kulturstudier, Box 1010 Blindern, N–0315 Oslo, Norway. E-mail: bjarne.rogan@iks.uio.no.

Introductory remarks

The following discussion springs from two different but linked problems. The first is how to cope with the phenomenon of passion in cultural analysis. The second is the concepts of symbol and symbolism and their use in ethnology. Research on private collectors and collecting has confronted me with an amazingly rich forest of "symbols" (in a wide sense of the term, including comparisons, metaphors, metonomies, parallelisms...) that compare collecting to passion, love and eroticism. These rhetorical figures, used in common parlance as well as in literary texts, might conveniently be termed symbols and the use of them symbolism, and then further discussion could be dropped. However, this would be unsatisfactory for two reasons. First, there is a bewildering diversity and lack of precision in the use of these terms by ethnologists. Second, there is a *systematic* use of "symbols" in my material that invites for further reflexion.

The material stems partly from my own indepth interviews with circa 50 collectors, with collections ranging from bric-a-brac and "instant collectibles" to books, coins and fine art, and partly from biographical sources, written statements in collectors' magazines, etc., and – not least – fiction.

The first and longest section of the article is a presentation and discussion of some empirical finds from my study of collecting, the second discusses symbols and symbolism, and the final tries to build a bridge between the two. Before embarking on this journey, the reader deserves a quick glimpse of the passionate collectors that constitute the empirical basis for the later discussions. The first quotation is from fiction – where an American collector of Indian wicker baskets is chatting to a casual listener – and the second from an interview with a Danish collector of folk art:

"Listen, pal, he says with a wink, you stand Brigitte Bardot next to a museum quality Tlingit [basket] and I wouldn't see her. I got a real nice Tlingit, by the way, got it at auction for eighteen bucks. A steal. It's worth much more. Pretty scarce" (Connell 1974:38).

"From time to time I have found something that I *had* to have, but that I couldn't afford. I have waited as much as twenty years to have the chance to acquire certain objects. Then I have been awake all night, sitting and just looking at it. It's just like being recently engaged to be married. There is a need for that experience – something that may make people believe that you are *erotically taken in* by the object [*object-erotoman*]. That's what I am, actually! I may become quite excited; many times your emotional life towards such an object is more intense than towards another person. It's not exactly the same feeling as falling in love, but the intensity is the same [...] "(Jacobsen, in Ohrt og Seisbøll 1992:73, transl. BR)

In addition to the discourse on collecting and eroticism, to be investigated here, there is a related discourse on collecting and madness, covering the whole field from frenzy to lunacy. Collectors tend to joke and flirt with their inclinations and talk humorously about their "disease" or "insanity". A quick look in dictionaries reveals that collectors are commonly considered *passionate, obsessive,* filled with *immoderate desire*, or – on the other side of the Channel – *passionné, fervent, obsédé, forcéné, féroce, maniaque,* in their *passion insatiable* for objects – and they may suffer from *une collectionnite aiguë.* Even if this discourse may blend with the erotic one, it will seldom qualify as "symbolic", as it is widely known that quite a few collectors only too easily transgress moral and legal boundaries and upset family economy and personal relations in their hunt for desired objects. The image of the slightly mad collector lies at the bottom of the recurrent use of them in media, in entertainment programs as well as for advertisements. Last year French TV screened a publicity sketch for a lottery; a collector scraped a ticket, found that he had won Ff 5.000 – and glued it on a wall that was already crammed with other tickets, with the comment: "Dammit, another copy of the same ticket!" The sketch works because people know that collectors' madness surpasses most other eccentricities.

If this is a common image of the collector, then why not leave the topic to psychologists and psychiatrists, who – by the way – also take a professional interest in symbols and symbolism? The answer is that collecting is normal behaviour, actually so normal that nearly one third of the adult population in countries like the US, the UK and France takes part in it, or has done so during periods of their adult lives (Attali 1989, Belk 1995, Pearce 1995). Also, some 90% of all schoolchildren collect. This presupposes a broad definition of collecting, but there is no reason to doubt that the percentage of persons practising some sort of collecting is approximately the same in most western countries. And among one third of the population there will always be a good number of borderline cases, which does not exclude the cultural analyst from the field. (For a thorough discussion of collecting from a psychological point of view, see Muensterberger 1994.)

The reader should be warned that the following discussion will draw the portrait of a collecting male. This does not mean that only men collect. Women probably practise collecting to the same extent that men do. Still, the idea that collecting is a masculine activity prevails, among collectors as well as in society in general. This idea is especially persistent in the popular discourse on collecting and eroticism. (For a discussion of gender and collecting, see Belk 1995, Pearce 1995, Rogan 1996.)

Passion and eroticism in collecting

A note on collectors and collecting in fiction

In his anthology *Breasts* (1993 and earlier ed.) Ramón Gómez de la Serna presents an artful, subtle and condensed sketch named The Collector. In spite of its brevity, it communicates many themes for an analysis of collecting; a creative gaze and a sense of aestheticism, the play aspect and the thrill of the find, a good portion of passion and a tinge of madness, an erotic loading and a certain possessiveness, a male and masculine activity with a stamp of absurdity, irrationality and futility – and the perishability of the collection. Here in a slightly abridged version:

"There is a lady asking for you, Sir", says the female servant to the collector of breasts [...]

"Let her in", says the collector, while adapting his position in the office chair in order to find a suitable angle and distance for the examination, as if adjusting his opera glasses.

The woman had delicate features and slender arms. Everything about her was graceful, but her breasts were so opulent that they seemed to greet the collector even before she had the time to reach out her hand with well-groomed nails.

"What can I do for you?", he asks.

"Well, to be honest ... You are a collector of breasts, aren't you? Well, here are mine ..."

The collector regretted not having his collector's glasses at hand to put them immediately on his nose, but compensated by leaning backwards in the chair [...]

The woman who offered her breasts unbuttoned her dress, like a wet nurse demonstrating the quality of her milk to the doctor.

The collector, who was used to demonstrations like this, touched the breasts that were offered him, carefully like a jeweller, while smiling entranced.

"Exceptional breasts for my collection! You bring me magnificent breasts. Unforgettable! You see ... It is important for me to have the possibility of looking at them when I want to, when I call them to my mind ... I cannot encase them in an album. On the other hand, I can call for you when I need these two beautiful items of my collection ..."

"You won't deceive me?", she said with coquetry.

"No ... They are the best of my collection .... I shall give them ten marks on a certificate that you can show everywhere ... Take care of them, take good care of them. The most beautiful breasts in my collection have disappeared or deteriorated from one day to the next."

An American trophy collector. From an American magazine, reproduced in *Samlarnytt* no 3–4/1959.

"I shall be careful with them, if not for any other reason than to offer them to you again ... Nobody treats them so gently and with so much tenderness as you do ... I am very satisfied ... Your certificate will always fill me with pride ..."

[...] The collector wrote in a ledger: "[Name, adr.] ... Buxom and delicate at the same time ... No drooping: The only breasts to my knowledge that, even if copious, don't have any trace of wrinkles or shadows, nor yet the slightest shadow of a beginning ruin and drooping [...] They are so serene and so beautiful that one does not feel the need to touch them" (de la Serna 1993:28–30. Transl. BR).

Authors of fiction are free to conjecture and interpret phenomena and invent realities that the researcher may perceive but hardly can document in a traditional way. The researcher may use fiction as a gateway to the popular interpretation and comprehension of phenomena. It may serve as his eyeopener to a symbolic world that is perhaps closed to those who use only traditional tools and sources. I shall rely heavily on fiction to be able to discuss symbolic aspects of collecting, aspects that are visible in my ordinary sources but most often more elusive and less direct than in the case of the Danish collector quoted above.

Before the 19th century collectors appear only sporadically in fiction. But with the rise of modern consumerism, industrialization and the spread of tastes and activities formerly reserved for the upper classes, collecting spreads to broader strata and increasingly finds its way into fiction. The most celebrated "collector novels" of the 19th century are *Le cousin Pons* (1847) by Honoré de Balzac and *Bouvard et Pécuchet* by Gustave Flaubert (1880/81), but the phenomenon of collecting is encountered in prose and poetry on both sides of the Atlantic. Around the turn of the century, a series of great American collectors – often called "robber barons" because they vacuumed Europe for art and antiquities – are portrayed in the novels of Theodore Dreiser, Henry James and Frank Norris. In afterwar years, American novelists like Evan S. Connell, Bruce Chatwin and Susan Sontag have depicted and analysed collectors, and so have also English John Fowles, French Georges Perec and German Nobel prize winner Elias Canetti. The list is far from exhaustive.

The collectors described are almost exclusively men. Collecting appears as a male and even virile activity. The quotation from de la Serna presented a collector of female breasts; Fowles' collector changes from butterflies to a woman, and Sontag's includes a beautiful woman in his collection of art and antiquities. The corollary of strong passions is chaos and destruction, and collecting offers no exception. Fowles' collector ends up by killing his "item", whereas Canetti's burns his collection. Sontag's novel is constructed around the volcano metaphor, with all the excesses, outbreaks and disasters that this implies.

"Passion and eroticism" turn out to be a central theme in these literary interpretations of collectors, as well as in other material. This overall theme may conveniently be presented in "phases": 1) Passion and desire, 2) Hunt and conquest, 3) Eroticism and power, and 4) Loss of control and transgression. In the following paragraphs these subthemes will be seen as symbolic representations, and not as sexual or other compensation. Admittedly, the latter interpretation would not contradict popular belief, but it may easily revert into pseudo-psychoanalysis (and is no longer in accordance with modern psychoanalytic understanding of collecting; cf. Formanek 1994)

For my literary examples I shall concentrate upon two novels, Balzac's *Le cousin Pons* (1847) and Sontag's *The Volcano Lover* (1992). There is a century and a half between them, and their authors' positions are as different as can be; on the one hand a French male realist – called the founding father of literary realism – looking at his own time; on the other hand a female American feminist and psychoanalytically oriented postmodernist looking back at history. But they are both "symbolists" in their interpretations of the collector. A few words will be appropriate to situate their novels.

In his fictional world – his *La Comédie Humaine* consisted of some one hundred novels – Balzac sets up what he called a sociological, anthropological and psychological inventory of virtues, vices and passions of his day, in order to give an exhaustive description of contemporary customs and usages. For a materialist (he excels in the description of objects) and a lover of modern society like Balzac, the collector was an ideal protagonist in a world of things. For him, collecting was both a means to realize aesthetic values and an arena for greed and evil. In short, the collector was the ideal tool "to chart virtues and vices" and "to collect the most important data about passion", as his program of literary realism ran.

For Susan Sontag also, the collector is a medium for saying something about man and society. Her protagonist moves from a purely aesthetic collecting project to a state of egoism, selfishness and insensibility to the suffering of others, his strongest passion being the emotional attachment to things. Persons (who, as a consequence, are never named) and things become indistinguishable and perish. The quest for the beautiful may end in hell, especially for collectors, who in the last resort collect themselves. Passion, possessiveness, betrayal, oblivion and destruction are her themes.

Two authors, two different literary traditions, and two different attitudes. For progressive and materialistic Balzac, collecting serves as a neutral activity to depict both positive and negative aspects of society. For postmodern Sontag, describing collectors is a means to unveil inhumanity, crumbling and decay, and a lack of coherence and continuity. Still, their metaphors and images are sometimes surprisingly similar – especially when it comes to collecting, passion and eroticism.

Love, passion and desire

"I fell smack in love with an old bread tray formed like a pig", recounted a female collector of antiquities (F, b. 1942). Not only female collectors use such terms. Norwegian men, who do not too often use terms like *love, covet, long for, desire, infatuated with* when the object is another person, surprisingly often fall back on these terms when talking about their collections. "Love makes blind", as the saying goes, and this is no less true for passionate collectors:

"If you are just passionate, you do one blunder after the other. If you are driven by love only [and lack knowledge], you get so infatuated that you do what I did, when I made a fool of myself by buying that tobacco box [a "Norwegian antiquity" that turned out to be a recent Russian box]. Nothing but love for the design! I lost my head completely. [...] On the other hand, if you didn't fall in love from time to time, if you never made any mistakes [...] If you keep going all life with a safety net, you will miss the thrill. [...] Love was so great that I didn't heed my intuition" (M, b. 1948).

Collectors' declarations of love are so numerous that we hardly need support from fiction on this point. However, passion and desire being the ubiquitous emotions of our two novels, greeting the reader from nearly every page, a passage from each would be appropriate:

"Paris is the city of the world that conceals most eccentrics [i.e. collectors], people with a religion in their heart. The eccentrics of London always end up by getting tired of their love affairs, just as they get tired of living. In Paris, however, the monomaniacs cohabit happily with their fantasies. You see them all the time, people like Pons and Elie Magus. They are dressed like paupers [...] They don't seem to care about anything, not about women, not about the warehouses. They seem to stroll at random, evidently without a penny and apparently absentminded and stupid [...] But these men, they are millionaires, collectors, the most passionate people in this world" (Balzac 1847/1956:135, transl. BR).

"As a child he collected coins, then automata, then musical instruments. Collecting expresses a free-floating desire that attaches and reattaches itself – it is a succession of desires. The true collector is in the grip not of what is collected but of collecting. [...] With the Cavaliere any passion sought the form of, was justified by becoming, a collection" (Sontag 1992:24, 27).

In Sontag's *The Volcano Lover*, fire-spitting Vesuvius serves both as the ominous background and as a potent metaphor for the uncontrollable collector's mania. The use of the volcano metaphor for a collector's passion is not new. In my interviews several respondents have used corresponding "eruptive" images. Best, however, is a French collector of sad-irons and founder and chairman of an international collectors' club, *Le club des amis des fers à repasser anciens.* He tells that he became a passionate collector at the age of 58, when his wife offered him an old iron. At the age of 74 this passion was still "a volcano which never stopped erupting since that time" (Bayart 1982). Indeed an appropriate metaphor, ten years before the publication of Sontag's novel.

Hunt and conquest

"Envy the adventures we have while on The Hunt. [...] But mostly envy us for The Thrill of The Find" exclaims an American "pack rat" or collector of bric-a-brac and curiosities (quoted after Belk 1995:72). An essential constituent of collecting is the hunt, and most items in most collections carry their proper history – of how they were conquered and incorporated in the collection. When interviewing collectors much of the conversation, sometimes the bulk of it, is about the acquisition of the various items: the unexpected find, the good buy, the shrewd bargaining, the clever bidding at the auction, the poking around at the flea market, the thrill of knowing more than the dealer, etc.

The collector's narrative is a predictable one: how and where they found the various items, how much they paid for them, and their real value and scarcity – in short: the treasure hunt. The following two cases, told by a knife collector (M, b. 1943), are typical, though the style a bit more juicy than the average:

"This knife [a precious 19th century item, handle carved in walrus tooth, engraved silver ornaments, signed by the artisan] – I came across it in Drammen. It was a steal! [...] I got it from a second hand dealer who didn't know what he was selling. He had to have a thousand crowns for it, he said. Man, he must be off his nut, I thought – all I can do is conclude the deal faster than the devil! I put the bill in his hand quick as lightning."

"This one [19th century knife, patriotic romantic style, handle and sheath carved in pukkenholtz] I got it from an antique dealer [...] He rang me up from a restaurant in Oslo. He was broke and half drunk, and needed money for a thorough soaking. [...] I jumped into the car, met him at the restaurant and got it for five thousand crowns. Then he could go on quenching his thirst with pints of beer. [...] Today you'll have to pay three or four times as much for it."

These narratives shift between the humourous and the serious, even the solemn. Some may imply a breach of rules, legal or moral, others may even have unintended religious overtones – like the collector who threw away his crutches during the hunt:

"My chum Peter is at least as crazy [a collector] as I am. [...] First time we met was in a container [where both of them were hunting for objects]. One afternoon we had a car trip – Peter, me and my dear Liza – who is just as mad as me. I suffer from sciatica, and that day I needed crutches because my left leg wouldn't come along. Before the trip Liza had whispered to Peter, without me hearing it: "Just wait until he sees a container. That'll heal him." When we came down the Wergelandsveien we spotted two containers, side by side on the sidewalk. I stopped short, got out of the car and ran for the containers – without my crutches!" (M, b. 1947).

Several respondents tell how they look out dealers who are *not* specialists in their own collecting fields, how they circle around in the shops, pretending to ignore or not take any genuine interest in those objects that immediately catch their attention – things that "speak loud to me" (M, b. 1948). No respondent, however, has described this play better than our two novelists. Balzac's narrative of how Pons conquered Madame de Pompadour's fan shows how the author – himself an ardent collector of antiquities – must have been a cunning and devious customer in antiquarians' shops. He describes the collector in his element, having discovered the desired object and entering a hand to hand combat for it, depreciating it and concealing his own knowledge of its real value. "Much experience is required to do a bargain like that", he states; "It's a combat face to face, where you look straight into the other's eye. And what a glance they have, these Jews and dealers from Auvergne!" (Balzac 1847/1956:35–36, transl. BR). To close this section on cunning and cautious hunters, we will leave the floor to Susan Sontag:

"That tremor when you spot it. But you don't say anything. You don't want to make the present owner aware of its value to you; you don't want to drive up the price, or make him decide not to sell at all. So you keep cool, you examine something else, you move on or you go out, saying you'll be back. You perform a whole theatre of being a little interested, but not immoderately; intrigued, yes, even tempted; but not seduced, bewitched. Not ready to pay even more than is being asked, because you must have it.

So the collector is a dissembler, someone whose joys are never unalloyed with anxiety. Because there is always more. Or something better" (Sontag 1992:71–72).

Eroticism and power

"The unmarried collector [...] sorts his mistresses according to style, period, or his artistic temperament", states Maurice Rheims in his essay on the strange life of objects (1959:21–22). Also, some collectors may themselves be quite outspoken on the subject of their relation to objects, cf. the Danish collector quoted in the introductory paragraph. But even if many of them talk openly about their collector's mania, overt erotic overtones are not so frequently heard in their own narratives. But some join in, like this collector of old silver and antiquities:

"To be hunting for an object and then get it – the comparison is a little hackneyed perhaps – but it's like being out fishing. It's exciting to hook the fish. Once you've got it into the boat, it's over. It's very much like that. It's sort of an orgasm. Suddenly it's over" (M, b. 1940).

When we turn to fiction, the material is overwhelming. There is but a short step from the passionate conquest of the object to the erotic conquest, if we are to believe numerous literary descriptions. de la Serna's collector of female attributes was described in an artful, allegorical form, whereas others are more direct. Balzac was of the opinion that the sum of passions in man was constant; a person with a very strong passion for collecting could hardly harbour other forms of love. Alternatives were scarce for unmarried Pons, "a person with beauty and refinement in his soul, but whose ugly appearance forbid any success with women" (1847/1956:7, transl. BR). We encounter a similar compensational idea in Sontag – "Obsessive collectors – natural bachelors" (1992:19) – and with several other authors. But both Balzac and Sontag pursue their play on words so far that the reader gets in doubt whether collecting is to be understood as compensation or as an erotic experience in itself:

"[Elie Magus] melted by the sight of a great work of art, like a libertine who is tired of women comes to life when seeing a young, beautiful girl and indulges in the hunt for flawless beauties. This Don Juan of paintings, this devoted admirer of perfection [...] lived in a harem of beautiful paintings. "

"When [Elie Magus] came across a work of art to his taste, his life changed; a haul was to be done, a transaction to be carried through, a great battle to be won. By hook and crook he went to work, and no tricks were left untried in order to bring home as cheap as possible the new woman of his harem."

"Pons and Magus carried in their hearts the same jealousy. [...] To get the chance to inspect the collection of [Pons] filled Elie Magus with the elated sens of happiness that is experienced only by a woman chaser who manages to enter the bedroom of the beautiful mistress that his friend tries to hide from him" (Balzac 1847/1956:131, 134, 137, transl. BR).

With Balzac, comparison alternates with metaphor. With Sontag, collecting and eroticism merge:

"Correggio's art. And Venus's groin. You can really possess – even if only for a little while. [...] There are so many objects. No single one is that important. There is no such thing as a monogamous collector. Sight is a promiscuous sense. The avid gaze always wants more."

"Collecting is a species of insatiable desire, a Don Juanism of objects in which each new find [...] generates the added pleasure of scorekeeping, of enumeration. Volume and tirelessness of conquest would lose some of its point and savior were there not a ledger somewhere [...] the happy contemplation of which at off-moments counteracts the exhaustion of desire that the erotic athlete is condemned to and against which he struggles."

"He yielded gratefully to the experience of satiety. Inevitably, some of his collecting zeal began to abate. [...] The collecting desire *can* be enfeebled by happiness – acute enough, erotic enough happiness – and the Cavaliere was happy, as happy as that" (Sontag 1992:71, 202, 180).

The collector and Don Juan are male social roles. No wonder, as only men are expected to openly show passion, to desire and to conquer. The erotic aspect of collecting may be given a concrete meaning, as in the case of the collector who kept "a ledger" of his memories of erotic adventures (cf. Belk 1995). As a metaphor it may represent an anthropomorphization of the object (cf. the Danish collector), or it may mean an objectification of the woman – as in Sontag (1992:138): "So the old man collected the young woman; it could not have been the other way around." But in any case, the harem and the Don Juanism of objects are metaphors that can be applied to any collector and any collection. Every collector wants more – just like any Don Juan. And all collections consist of series of objects – like a harem. Vittorio Fellini hit the mark when he let his male collector in *Citta della Donne* collect women's underpants!

A harem connotes more than eroticism. It also means power and control. "There is hardly a more absolute ruler in a secret harem than a man amidst his objects", says Baudrillard (1969:125). It is a common interpretation that collecting attracts because the collection represents a closed universe where its master rules unconditionally. The collector God imposes order and system in his little private world.

The collector bestows economic and moral value on his objects, simply by incorporating them in the collection. The collector must have a certain position, self-esteem and self-confidence. A status of connoisseur transfers a corresponding status to the objects. Thanks to their traditionally strong position in the world of production and economic values, men more than women have a status that conveys connoisseurship. "... collecting was still a virile occupation", Sontag writes (1992:22); "It stemmed from a lordly sense of himself that Catherine – indeed, all but very few women – could not have." Allegedly, men confirm their own images through their collections, just as they may strengthen their self image through erotic conquests. This argument leads to the mirror metaphor: a collection functions as a mirror where the collector sees what he wants to see (cf. Rheims 1959, Baudrillard 1969, Stewart 1984, Clifford 1988, Pearce 1995). That this image may contribute to an understanding of the self that is not only agreeable, is a topic for the next paragraph.

Transgression, loss of control and chaos

To collect is a passion that may end up as a vice. Many respondents compare collecting to alcoholism, gambling or drug addiction: the passion may be controlled, but there is also a chance that economic and moral rules are broken and fortunes lost. To start with the most concrete risks, we shall listen to the advice of an experienced collector of curiosities:

"You must make a few deals with yourself and keep control over your collecting. If you know about markets coming up, put aside money beforehand, as I do. You must be strict with yourself. It's like alcohol. I know many persons who went to the dogs because they couldn't draw the line. [...] That's why I have managed a fairly long life both as a user of alcohol and as a collector. [...] You can't let love surpass reason too often. Then you'll squander everything. You must draw the line" (M, b. 1948).

Good advice of course, but temptations lurk everywhere for a collector. Newspapers are all too full of reports on thefts, faking and court trials where collectors are implicated, and the narratives of the (male) respondents abound with stories of purchases where months' wages are spent – sometimes even of "innocent borrowing". "They are willing if needs be to risk prosecution to have an old cup, a painting, a rare object", Balzac wrote in 1847 (1956:135).

"Every collector is potentially (if not actually) a thief", is the harsh comment from Susan Sontag 150 years later (1992:73). "There seems to exist a special morality for collectors, who are driven by an irresistible desire to complete the collection", wrote August Strindberg (1910) and went on: "Even the most upright among bibliophiles is a potential danger to himself and to others"; "Yes, I had to have that folio, or die", is the Strindbergian collector's concession to the judge on the accusation of theft. When passions are strong, temptations become numerous.

But the collector's transgression has consequences beyond these breaks of formal rules and of social decency, consequences of a more abstract and personal kind. Sontag is strongly preoccupied with destructive and self-destructive aspects of collecting, and her protagonist moves closer and closer to the edge of the vomiting crater. The volcano metaphor works on several levels; Vesuvius is the unique and unownable object that the collector is constantly longing for; and it stands for the collector himself, unpredictable and destructive in his passion; it also reminds us of the uncontrollable forces of Passion itself; and it conveys an image of the collector's self-contempt in rare moments of self-examination, including a longing for self-destruction. A collector balances on the border of the unknown, of his own destructive forces, of his own abolition:

"Like passion, whose emblem it is, it can die. [...] The river of fire, after consuming all in its path, will become a river of black stone. Trees will never again grow here, ever. The mountain becomes the graveyard of its own violence: the ruin the volcano causes includes its own" (Sontag 1992:7).

The very excessiveness of the collecting passion makes the collector a self-despiser, she claims; the collector is preoccupied with the idea of preservation and conservation and at the same time he is a thief and a robber; he is a lover of beauty and an extreme materialist. These contradictions give collectors a divided consciousness – which may lead to a longing to be purged by a consuming fire, for a holocaust that may relieve him of his collection. Or so goes her argument (1992:187) – not without a strong resonance of both Freud and Baudrillard (1968:149–50). Similar thoughts may be traced in other novels; Canetti's book-collector ends up by burning his collection, and Fowles' collector kills his most desired object, the girl. But to quote Sontag again: "... should such an angry collector survive his fire or fit, he will probably want to start another collection."

The collector's self-contempt at moments may of course be due to the clash between his sense of aesthetics and his strong materialism, as Sontag proposes. However, collecting seems to offer precisely a socially acceptable form of materialism in modern consumer society, according to recent research (Belk 1995), and this is probably another reason why collecting is considered good entertainment. Perhaps Walter Benjamin, himself a book-collector, offers a better clue with his idea of collecting as a dialectic process between order and chaos:

"For what is this possession [the collection] other than chaos, where habit has become so much a part of it that it appears as order? You have heard about people who fell ill by the loss of their books, and about others who have become criminals through their activity. Any order in this field is nothing but an existence on the edge of an abyss [...] Thus, the collector's existence is dialectically extended between the poles of disorder and order" (Benjamin 1972, transl. BR).

All passion approaches chaos, Benjamin states, collecting however the chaos of memory. Contemplating his books when unpacking his library, he observed that chance and destiny were overwhelmingly present in his collection. Any collection requires systematizing, i.e. order, but it also serves as a monument of the arbitrary life of the collector. Through the memories that are conveyed by each object, the collector is constantly confronted with his past – a past that in the case of Benjamin was marked by chance more than planning, by disorder more than order. As a collector, he found himself hovering above the abyss of memory.

In my field work I have met two or three collectors who actually have signalled a certain weariness – in one case almost distaste – with their collections. The latter one was strongly addicted to collecting, a person for whom collecting was far more important than what he collected. During a two hours inspection of an enormous collection that literally filled attics, basement and garages, or rather five or six very unsystematic collections ranging from consumer's everyday items to old paintings, from advertisement posters and old tin cans to vintage cars, my cicerone gradually became less enthusiastic. At the end of the visit, he suddenly looked at me with a weary gaze that told more than words, adding: "Sometimes I get a feeling of dullness and fatigue. It's too much!" (M, b. 1957).

We have apparently moved away from our main subject, eroticism. But Sontag takes us back. In her symbolic world, the collector's self-understanding and feeling of satiety and excess has a parallel in eroticism:

"Like sexual feelings, when they become a focus of dedication or devotion, and are actually lived out in all their vehemence and addictiveness, so the feeling for art (and beauty) can, after a while, only be experienced as excess, as something that strains to surpass itself, to be annihilated. To really love something is to wish to die of it. Or to live only in it, which is the same thing. To go up and never have to come down" (Sontag 1982:340).

We have now moved – analytically – through the different phases of the collector's passion; from the falling in love and the desire for the object, through the hunting and the conquest to the erotic aspects, to end up with loss of control, chaos and self-examination. Before the final discussion of this figurative or metaphorical world – or should we call it symbolic? – we must decide what we mean by terms like symbolic and symbolism.

Some remarks on symbols and symbolism

To those who believe that the debate on symbols and symbolism may be based on a few simple definitions one may retort that every definition is relative, states Daniel Fabre. He compares the researcher of symbolism to an explorer of regions increasingly unknown, sometimes hesitating to move on and constantly in search of instruments to find his bearings in a strange territory (1989:61). The following brief outline, with all its biases and shortcomings, is a necessary step in this study – in order to understand a rather obscure part of the history of our discipline, and to make clear my own position in relation to a long and sinuous history of symbol studies. It is, to quote Fabre, a search for instruments to find one's bearings.

Concepts and traditions

The cultural analyst who wants to bring order into the use of concepts like symbol, symbolism and symbolic understanding, is likely to break his neck for obvious reasons: there are so many different definitions and traditions, disciplinary as well as national; disciplines have borrowed from each other and made adaptations; and there is a lack of unanimity even within the various disciplines. The problem is not only the concepts and the vocabulary, but also a lack of consensus as to what is actually the object of study. There is a tradition – not least within European ethnology – for a restricted acceptation of symbolism, aiming at the analysis of various elements of culture, or "symbols", with an immediately expressive or communicative content. And there is another acceptation of symbolism, or symbolic understanding, that is much wider, implying the study of the attribution of meaning through the culture's classification of the objects in the world (Lenclud 1991). In this wide acceptation of symbolism, at least, we are still "explorers in a strange and unknown world".

Another important opposition in studies of symbolism is that of meaning versus function, or very schematic: what symbols say and what symbols do. In the first case, the analysis deals with contents, logic or structural properties of the symbolic systems, which are studied in a cognitive or communicative context. In the second case, the studies concentrate on social, religious and political functions; the symbolic systems (where rituals play an important part) are investigated in their instrumental aspects and interpreted in relation to organisation and domination. The latter trend in symbol studies has found its most fertile soil in Durkheimian anthropology of religion and in functional anthropology in the Radcliffe-Brown tradition (Lenclud 1991). As the present study of collecting focuses on meaning and structural properties, nothing more will be said here about the functionalist approach.

Linguistics and semiotics (semiology) have furnished the cultural disciplines with the concepts of sign and symbol. The two mutually different *sign*-concepts, handed down from F. de Saussure and W. Sanders Peirce, seem to be the only concepts that are not subject to much disagreement. But as we move on from sign to *symbol* definitions start to diverge, even between and within the various semiotic traditions, for instance as to the relationship between sign and symbol, whether the symbol is an arbitrary or a partly motivated sign, etc. All the divergent symbol concepts in semiotics, literary theory and language philosophy (cf. Eco 1984) taken into consideration, the confusion around these two concepts in our own discipline is hardly surprising. Readers of recent issues of *Ethnologia Europaea* will have met with circumlocutions like "the signs/symbols which ... ", "the motives/symbols of the flag ...", "the most prominent signs and symbols ...", etc. – in otherwise recommendable articles. On a more official level, this somewhat awkward state of affairs became evident last year when German ethnologists arranged their biennial conference, the subject of which was announced as: *Symbole – zur Bedeutung der Zeichen in der Kultur* ("Symbols – On the Meaning of Signs in Culture"). The arrangers had to coin a title where both sign and symbol appeared, and the reality behind this is more than a terminological problem.

However, my material on collecting, as discussed on the preceding pages, does not lend itself to an analysis of sign and symbols in a restricted sense (whatever they are), so I shall not undertake the risky task of proposing (pragmatic) workable definitions. Also, as I find no support in traditional semiotics for an analysis of the systematic symbolic aspects of my material, I shall look to competing anthropological theories. This means that I will include metaphors, allegories and other rhetorical figures in my conception of symbolism as a mode of thinking, in accordance with most anthropological theories but contrary to e.g. Eco's semiotic symbol theory (1984).

Traditions from psychoanalysis have also had their impact on our discipline's pragmatic use and understanding of symbols and symbolism. (I here disregard the oldest psychoanalytic tradition of investing symbols with one single, universal meaning, as opposed to the relativist interpretations of anthropology.) This double heritage from linguistics and psychoanalysis uncovers a considerable paradox. Both traditions would contend that the basic meaning of a symbol is an object, an activity, an expression etc. that represents something else. But whereas the paramount interest from the linguistic/semiotic point of view is interpersonal communication, the psychoanalyst is mainly interested in the opposite function, the symbol as a substitute for something else that is hidden to the individual, its function being to conceal repressed ideas to his consciousness. In short, we have to do with either communication or censorship, or with conscious versus unconscious use of symbols. Both traditions have had their impact on and been practised in ethnology/anthropology, another reason why some of us have felt it difficult to reach a deeper understanding of the field. Even if part of my material from fiction is influenced by psychoanalytic ideas, a further investigation in this direction will imply a discussion of unconscious symbols and (sexual) compensation. This perspective is by no means irrelevant when it comes to understanding collecting, but to force the overall material into a compensation theory would mean undue reductionism.

The sign vs. symbol complex, a major concern in the tradition of the restricted acceptation of symbolism (see above), is only one part of the linguistic lesson to anthropology. The linguistic basis lead to a perception of symbolism as a *system* of symbols, rather than a series of isolated symbols (as in the old Freudian tradition). This insight found its utmost expression in structural anthropology, as demonstrated by Claude Lévi-Strauss, whose analysis concentrated upon the formal and logic organisation of symbols more than on the content of meaning in the separate symbols. Precisely this systematic aspect of symbolism has attracted my attention, as it gives an opportunity to discuss the systematic character of the metaphors that I have met in the material on collecting. Structuralism, taken as a philosophy or as a scientific method, has been subject to severe criticism for a couple of decades, and rightfully. But as "a way of seeing things", to quote Edmund Leach, structuralism can still contribute to the study of culture.

The metaphoric / metonymic principle – a structuralist approach

I have so far ignored one important element of the history of ethnology, viz. the discourse on primitive thought. Classification is indispensable for research, but at the risk of distorting perspectives or losing certain aspects. Ethnological research, not least in museums, have tended to systematize cultural material in categories, under headings like agriculture, costumes, food and diet, crafts and trades, etc. But there was a series of phenomena that escaped classification, or rather were put together in one box: objects, words and deeds, attitudes, ideas and conceptions that referred to beliefs, superstition, symbolism – or whatever this heterogenous leftover category was called. That symbolism is an aspect that intersects all empirical categories is a modern insight.

Researchers were of course children of their time, and the heritage from evolutionism was tenacious. Habits, opinions and popular interpretations that did not fit in with scientific thinking was far into the afterwar period seen as a sign of irrationality, something that marked "The Other", whether a native in a primitive culture or a primitive (= peasant) in our own culture. Collected popular culture material indicated that humanity was divided in two: those who thought rationally, and those who thought symbolically.

The ethnologist's burden until fairly recently has been this idea of a division between two ways of thinking; the researcher's tool was the logical, rational way of thinking, as opposed to the prelogical or symbolic way, represented by his object of study. But it became increasingly difficult to maintain that humanity was divided in this way. Slowly it became clear that everyone, modern western man included, has the potential for both ways of thinking. But the researcher had been so well trained to repress symbolic thinking in his own mind, to the profit of rational thinking, that he was blind to the symbolic thinking in his own, civilized world. "The savage mind" or "la pensée sauvage", to borrow an expression from Lévi-Strauss, was everywhere.

This leads us to the provisional conclusion that symbolism is an alternative way of comprehending and interpreting the world. The great paradox for the researcher is that even if he acknowledges the existence in himself of a symbolic way of thinking, he has to formulate this insight by means of a logical, scientific language. But his best ally is the artist and author of fiction, who is free to do "research" and interprete things his way.

Yet we have not explained how symbols work. Let us lend an ear to the structuralist's explanation of the systematic character of signs in culture. When a concrete phenomenon – an object, an action, a narrative ... – may be perceived in a symbolic sense, i. e. as representing something else that it obviously is not from a realistic point of view, this must be due to some sort of similarity that makes possible a comparison of the two. This similarity cannot reside in substance, nor in form, as these are different by definition. There remains, however, the possibility for similarity or identity in structure, that is a structure that may repeat itself in different types of substance. Without endorsing all ideas and principles of structural anthropology (several of which must probably be discarded today), it seems apropriate to draw the attention to one of their basic postulates: that metaphorical cross-references between dissimilar cultural phenomena is possible only because their structures are identical. (NB: postulates do not only belong to prelogical thinking, as it used to be contended!)

The structuralist claimed that it is with culture as it is with natural languages, because language is part of culture: both are governed by a set of rules (a "grammar") and a system of classifications. The crown case is the similarities between eating and sexual behaviour. Rules, as much as biology, classify between what is eatable and not, and other rules tell us how and when and where to gather, prepare and eat the food. In every culture there is a "food grammar", as specialised and refined as any grammar – and dining etc. is a way of communicating, like talking. The paradigmatic axis (the "vertical" list of alternatives or interchangeable items) offers the metaphors, whereas the syntagmatic axis (the "horizonal" sequence, including proximity and context) caters for the metonomies. The same applies to the "grammar" for sexual comportment, with rules for what is permitted and what is not, who you can have a relation to, etc., i. e. distinctions that belong to culture, not to nature.

These two fields – of eating and of sexuality – are commonly referred to because they appear to be identical in structure. They have so many similarities that metaphorical cross-references are very common. This had been observed for a long time, in psychoanalysis as well as in functionalist anthropology. But it was structural anthropology that proposed an analysis that was far more sophisticated than that of Frazer, Radcliffe-Brown or Freud. Behind this analysis hides another postulate, viz. that the human mind, which creates all these systems and classifications, is in itself an entity that creates similar structures in all its products – be it languages, eating, sexuality, dreaming ... – and why not collecting?

Towards a conclusion

Collecting and structure – and so what?

Collecting covers a broad range of practices (from the taxonomic to the aesthetic way of collecting) and of activities (chasing, systematizing, exhibiting, studying ...), of aims and motivations, and of types of objects collected. No single, isolated symbolic expression can possibly capture this broad and varied field of activities. As shown in the first section, there is actually a surprising world of images associated with collectors and collecting, in everyday parlance and in popular opinion as well as in the artist's fictional world. These rhetorical figures are remarkable for three reasons: their high number, their systematic character, and because of all the cross-references between collecting and sexuality, or eroticism.

A close look at the discourse on collecting has revealed a long series of coherent and mutually interdependent metaphors and comparisons. In human experience these images represent elements that go together in a syntagmatic chain: passion and desire – chase and conquest – a concentration on what is unique and an unquenchable thirst for the series – masculinity and virility – power and egoism – satisfaction and satiety – transgression and destruction – and (perhaps) self-examination; things allowed and things unwarranted, things coveted and odious things – according to cultural rules.

The discourse on collecting links together two apparently very different fields of human activity. The act of collecting material objects is continually being compared to sexual comportment and referred to in terms of relations between the two sexes. Such linking represents a form of experience and a manner of expression that used to be associated with prelogical or symbolic thought, but that we now acknowledge as our own way of thinking also. And we might as well accept the formal explanation proposed by the structuralist, viz. that these cross-references are possible only because the human brain has structured these two fields of experience, as well as the language that we use to express them, in the same way.

However, formal structure can explain only why this linking is possible. But why do we select just eroticism as a parallell to collecting, and not other important spheres of activity? Which categories do the two fields have in common that are so important? Are there some basic human needs that find their expression primarily in these two spheres? And how to explain its almost universal character, as we find the same linking in most (or in all?) western cultures and languages?

So far we have concluded that the elaborate discourse on collecting and eroticism may be defined as symbolism, or symbolic understanding, at least in a formalist and structuralist meaning of the term. It is a recurrent problem, however, with analyses of formal aspects of culture that they very often push ahead of them the most interesting questions. I shall not pursue a lengthy (and probably speculative) discussion of these questions. I will instead close with a few remarks on the ambiguity of collecting, which may contain fragments of an answer.

Collecting – an ambiguous activity

There can be no doubt that *passion* and *desire* lie at the core of both collecting and eroticism. To insist on the role of passion in an erotic affair would be a waste of time. But the relationship between passion and collecting is worth while expanding on. We may contend that against passion for sexual gratification stands the collector's passion for possession. It is commonly thought that collecting represents the quintessence of possessing and the collector the embodiment of a possessor. By definition, a collector's item should be neither for practical use (in that case he is a user or a hoarder) nor *only* an economic investment (in that case he is an investor). An object is collected precisely because it is useless (= aesthetic or symbolic), and its function in a collection is simply to be possessed. "It was no longer the chase that obsessed him, but the sheer joy of ownership", says Sontag (1992:180). Baudrillard is outspoken on this point:

"Let us admit that our everyday objects actually are the objects of a passion – the passion for private possession. The emotional strength of this passion is by no means inferior to our passions for people. We experience this passion every day. Sometimes it has complete mastery over us, in the absence of other passions. As a passion our possessiveness is kept in balance, unclear, controlling – and we are hardly conscious of its basic role for the equilibrium of the individual and the group, even for the will to live. As such, [...] the objects are a mental fence that marks the borders of my kingdom; I am their ultimate meaning [...]" (Baudrillard 1968:120, transl. BR).

Thus passion and possession go together, just like passion and eroticism. In one case passion for objects, in the other passion for persons. The one may be as strong as the other, and this gives a platform for metaphors.

This dichotomy object–person is an important one. Let us return a last time to the images used, in fiction as well as in everyday language. There are 150 years between the author who wrote about the collector who "stared at the paintings as a lover looks at a mistress" (Balzac) and the modern newspaper journalist who wrote about a collector that "He collected stamps, while the rest of his classmates collected girls" (*Aftenposten* 28.4.1995). And Susan Sontag does not even bother to name her characters. People and things merge, and this is a central characteristic of all images used in the discourse on collecting and eroticism.

There weighs a basic ambiguity upon collecting, which may be explained as a clash between society's norms and the collector's practice, with reference to the oppositions people–things, immaterial–material and animate–inanimate. The discourse on collecting insists upon a basic similarity in our behaviour towards what is animate and what is inanimate. In spite of our humanistic ideals that make a sharp distinction between people and things, the collector overtly and publicly shows strong emotions for what is material and inanimate. According to our cultural norms (and also our logical, scientific thinking), emotions should be directed towards living creatures and spiritual values, not towards dead things. Still, in the emotional life of the avid collector distinctions between people and objects seem to be wiped out.

Because the collector openly defies society's ideology and norms (but not its mentality) through his materialism, he has become a focus of interest. To some, he plays the role of the clown; he is the fool who is accepted because he reminds us of our hypocrisy, that we are materialists without acknowledging it. Others will despise him and consider his activity (sexual) compensation or fetishism. But the majority seem to respect him and his activities because they feel a resonance of their own relationship to things, even if the difference in degree may be considerable. I venture that an important reason for the collector to attract so much attention is to be found in our ambiguity to materialism.

But can collecting be reduced to possessiveness and materialism only? Certainly not! In one of her novels, Tove Jansson lets the character Hemulen (collector of beetles and of stamps) complete a special collection. When realizing what had happened, his reaction was dismay and deep consternation for having become *only* an owner of stamps and not being a collector any longer! Collecting is also play, creativity and aesthetic practice – other characteristics that it has in common with eroticism. There seems to be no simple and unambiguous answer to our question why two important fields of human experience may symbolize each other.

References

Aftenposten 28.4.1995. Oslo.

Attali, Danielle 1989: *La passion des collections.* Paris.

Balzac, Honoré de 1956 (1847): *Le cousin Pons.* Paris.

Baudrillard, Jean 1969: *Le système des objets.* Paris.

Belk, Russel W. 1995: *Collecting in a Consumer Society.* London and New York.

Benjamin, Walther 1972 ff: *Gesammelte Schriften.* Frankfurt am Main.

Canetti, Elias 1963: *Die Blendung.* München.

Claverie, Elisabeth 1987: Les symbolismes majeures. In: Chiva, Isac & Utz Jeggle: *Ethnologies en miroir* Paris.

Clifford, James 1988: *The Predicament of Culture: Twentieth-century Ethnography, Literature and Art.* Cambridge, Mass.

Connell, Evan S. Jr. 1974: *The Connoisseur.* New York.

Eco, Umberto 1984: *Semiotics and the Philosophy of Language.* London.

Elsner, John and Roger Cardinal 1994 (eds.): *The Cultures of Collecting.* London.

Ethnologia Europaea.

Fabre, Daniel 1989: Le symbolisme en questions. In: Martine Segalen (ed.): *L'Autre et le semblable. Regards sur l'ethnologie des sociétés contemporaines.* Paris.

Flaubert, Gustave 1979 (1880/1881): *Bouvard et Pécuchet.* Paris.

Formanek, Ruth 1994: Why they collect. Collectors reveal their motivations. In: Susan Pearce: *Interpreting Objects and Collections.* London.

Fowles, John 1965 (1963): *The Collector.* London.

Frölich, Juliette 1993: Om mennesker og ting i romanen. *Samtid og fortid.* Museumsnettverket nr. 2. Oslo, Norges Forskningsråd.

Leach, Edmund 1970: *Claude Lévi-Strauss.* Oslo.

Lenclud, Gérard 1991: Symbolisme. In: *Dictionnaire de l'ethnologie et de l'anthropologie.* Paris.

Lévi-Strauss, Claude 1962: *La pensée sauvage.* Paris.

Muensterberger, Werner 1994: *Collecting: An Unruly Passion. Psychological Perspectives.* Princeton.

Hainard, Jacques et R. Kaehr (eds.) 1982: *Collections passion.* Neuchâtel.

Pearce, Susan 1994: *Interpreting Objects and Collections.* London.

Pearce, Susan 1995: *On Collecting: An Investigation into Collecting in the European Tradition.* London.

Perec, George 1978: *La vie mode d'emploi. Roman.* Paris.

Rheims, Maurice 1959: *La vie étrange des objets. Histoire de la curiosité.* Paris.

Rheims, Maurice 1992: *Apollon à Wall Street* Paris.

Rogan, Bjarne 1996: Et møtested for maskulin lidenskap og feminin estetikk? En foreløpig drøfting av kjønnsperspektiver ved samling. *Dugnad* vol. 22 no. 3. Oslo.

Samlarnytt. Organ för riksförbundet Nordstjärnan no 3–4/1959. Stockholm.

Serna, Ramón Gómez de la 1993: *Seins* (Transl. from Spanish to French). Marseille.

Sontag, Susan 1992: *The Volcano Lover: a Romance.* New York.

Stewart, Susan 1993 (1984): *On Longing. Narratives of the Miniature, the Gigantic, the Souvenir, the Collection.* Durham and London.